"*Beyond the Jordan* is a tapestry, beautifully woven. This book would sit well alongside Brian Doyle's *Book of Uncommon Prayer* or Ezekiel, Rumi, Rilke, or Jessie van Eerden. 'The weight of glory' suffuses these essays, via a cup of coffee, a desert flower, or a language lesson with a new friend. Most of all, *Beyond the Jordan* is an ode to faith and to the kinship we find in the places that call us home."

—**Joni Tevis**
Author of *The World Is on Fire*

"I have been waiting for this book, one that captures the Middle East that's not headline news: the Middle East of kite flying, olive farming, Bedouin weavers, and endless cups of tea. Heather Surls illuminates in lyrical prose the mandates of modern life while embedding them in this ancient land."

—**Mindy Belz**
Journalist, editor, and author of *They Say We Are Infidels: On the Run from ISIS with Persecuted Christians in the Middle East*

"All who love the lands of the Bible and wonder how the prophecies of old will ever come true are invited to sit with Heather and listen and learn and pray and wait for bitter waters to turn sweet. *Beyond the Jordan* is a spiritual memoir, a journalistic adventure, a love letter to the Middle East, a tribute to resilience, and a prophetic invitation to nurture hope."

—**Dr. Carmen Joy Imes**
Associate Professor of Old Testament at Talbot School of Theology and author of *Bearing God's Name: Why Sinai Still Matters*

Beyond the Jordan

Dry Places, Misunderstood Peoples, and Imperfect Attempts at Prayer

HEATHER M. SURLS

Artwork by Sarah Elizabeth Racine

LUCIDBOOKS

Earlier versions of these chapters appeared in the following magazines and journals:

"Beyond the Jordan" in *River Teeth*

"A Portrait of Baghdad as Beautiful" in *Silk Road*

"Slowly, Slowly" in *Brevity*

"Into the Rugged Unknown" in *Anthrow Circus* as "Shepherding Goats with a Jordanian Bedouin"

"Attention" in *LETTERS* as "Desert"

Portions of "Table in the Wilderness" in *Anthrow Circus* and *EthnoTraveler*

"Yet I Will Rejoice" in *Relief*

"On the Border" in *Nowhere*

"Sketches of Syrian Women" in *Belmont Story Review* as "Syrian Women"

"My Other Name Is Hagar" in *Vita Poetica*

Table of Contents

Preface

Dear Reader,

Life in the Middle East is incredibly dynamic. Since I finished the first complete draft of this manuscript in May 2024, Bashar al-Assad's regime fell in Syria, the war in Gaza reached a fragile ceasefire, and Donald Trump's return to the White House froze refugee resettlement. By the time you read these words, I'm sure there will be more significant developments. At the same time, I'm confident that the stories in your hands—mine and those of many, many Arab women—will be just as relevant as when I first wrote them.

"Who is an Arab?" you may be asking. Some consider anyone who speaks Arabic an Arab. Others prefer to define Arabs as descendants of nomads who came from Saudi Arabia and now populate vast portions of the Middle East and North Africa. When I use the term here, I'm usually referring to Arabic speakers from places such as Jordan, Syria, Palestine, and Iraq—people I live alongside here in the Hashemite Kingdom of Jordan.

My husband, Austin, and I moved here more than a decade ago so he could pursue work at a local seminary for Arab Christians, who comprise about 2 percent of Jordan and 5 percent of the Middle East. The seminary needed long-term faculty with PhDs, which Austin had, and we were eager to return to the region after living in Israel for two years. Since coming here, I have made a vast array of relationships through being neighborly, volunteering in refugee communities, and developing my career as a writer.

You'll meet many of these friends and acquaintances in the pages of *Beyond the Jordan*. If I interviewed someone as a journalist, his or her real name appears. However, the names of most others have been changed to conceal their identities and respect their cultural value of modesty. Most Arab Muslim women are extremely protective of their public identity and don't use their real names on social media or their faces in profile pictures.

Some of the stories you'll read in *Beyond the Jordan* will challenge you. Encountering unfamiliar perspectives, narratives, and voices can be uncomfortable. I hope you'll lean into the tensions you feel and allow any stereotypes you've unknowingly (or knowingly) embraced to be softened—stereotypes about Muslim women or Palestinians, for example, or even about the nature of faith.

If reading this book sparks in you a greater curiosity about Arabs and cultivates empathy for them as fellow human beings fashioned in the Creator's image, or if it invites you to press deeper into the majesty and mystery of God, I will consider *Beyond the Jordan* a success.

Grace & peace,
Heather M. Surls

INVOCATION

The Desert Will Bloom

I once walked a trail in northern Jordan, one infested with burrs and saw-toothed, spiral seed pods. It was a goat path, perhaps, scattered with marbles of dung, and the limestone hillside it threaded was planted with patches of olive and fig trees. In spite of the thistles and stones, I tromped forward, for there were flowers in the path too, pressing out of the cracked earth. It was early November; measurable rain had not fallen in months.

The flowers looked primordial, nascent, sets of palest pink petals coming right out of the dirt, without leaves or even stems. Scientifically, they're called colchicum. Their common names include meadow saffron, naked lady, and autumn crocus. They resemble the true crocus, germinating from bulb-like corms beneath the soil. There on the east-west trail in a region known as Gilead, the flowers were spaced a yard or two apart, sporadic yet frequent enough that I pursued them like a scavenger. They felt like signs egging me on toward a promise.

I followed the trail of colchicum until I knew why, until prophecies began to seep up from my mind's cistern. A whisper: *The desert and the parched land will be glad. The wilderness will rejoice and blossom.* I sat on a rock to listen as phrases and images burbled from a reservoir of words dug deep in my consciousness since my California childhood. A tractor growled ahead of me, a *muezzin* chanted behind me. I swatted at flies and little grasshoppers and focused to hear: *Like the crocus [the desert] will burst into bloom; it will rejoice greatly and shout for joy.*

Several months earlier, I'd spoken with Mustafa al-Shudeifat, program coordinator at Jordan's Royal Botanical Garden, in my work as a freelance journalist. Al-Shudeifat decried the popular conception of Jordan as a duned Sahara desert. Eighty percent of the nation receives standard desert levels of rain—less than four inches annually—yet he lauded the country's biodiversity. More than 5,000 plant species have been recorded in these 34,750 square miles, an area roughly the size of Indiana.

"Here in Jordan," he told me, "the people don't call the desert, *desert*. They call it *badia*—the living desert."

What hope, what belief I hear inherent in this one Arabic word, a distinct term for a desert that produces flora with only scant amounts of rain. I love how al-Shudeifat insisted on this word, how he defended his desert. He had experienced its potential while working in grazing-land rehabilitation projects. He had seen the badia's plants, knew how for centuries Bedouin nomads used this land for grazing their camels and goats. He knew that life could spring from apparently desperate dryness. He had seen colchicum rise.

And now I had discovered them, really seen colchicum for the first time. I returned to the goat trail with a pencil and attempted to sketch the flowers in the margins of Isaiah. *Water will gush forth in the wilderness and streams in the desert,* declared the prophet. Nearly 3,000 years ago, this man associated with Jewish kings in Jerusalem, possessing both the moxie of a revolutionary and the eloquence of a poet. *The burning sand will become a pool, the thirsty ground bubbling springs.*

These flowers reminded me of ones I'd seen in Wadi Rum in southern Jordan. My son David and I had climbed a canyon, rocks shifting and scraping beneath our feet like shale roof tiles gone loose. My husband, Austin, an Old Testament professor at a small Jordanian college, was bouldering ahead of us, searching for Edomite inscriptions. Beyond the carcass of a fox—only fur and bones left, sun-bleached teeth exposed, four clawed feet arranged like he'd fallen dead while running—we found a five-petaled flower glowing purple. It was a jolt to eyes accustomed to hours of variations on brown. Our Bedouin guide said Wadi Rum gets three to six days of rain a year. *How does this plant find strength to live in this sand?* I thought. *How does it resist and defy the elements?*

I experienced this same wonder while shadowing a Bedouin shepherd in the rugged mountains of the Dana Biosphere Reserve, also in southern Jordan. The farther Mohammad and I climbed up rocky ravines, which looked barren from afar, the more varieties of wildflowers I found. Most were small, clinging close to the ground, and many had thorns accompanying their blossoms. But they appeared step after step in bewildering variety. Gold coin. Egyptian bugloss. Rock rose. Spiny milkvetch. White broom. I stooped and pinched off flowers whenever I could. By the end of the day, my cardigan pockets were stuffed with wilted specimens.

3

As I meditated on Isaiah's words with the colchicum flowers at my feet, I realized they were harbingers, forerunners of a future reality. They—and all the flowers in this country, really—were little prophets jumping out of the dust and shouting at me, "Believe, and you will see the glory of God!"

Glory? Where is the glory here, in a region blowing up with headlines of terror and war, drought and poverty, refugees and intifadas, persecuted peoples, oppression, and oppressors? Most people don't recognize it, locals included. Regularly, when Arabs hear I'm American, they ask, "Then why are you living *here*?" Often I explain that my husband teaches at a seminary for Arabic-speaking Christians, that I'm a writer who enjoys helping Westerners understand Arabs more accurately. Sometimes I add that we value the conservative yet multicultural atmosphere in which we're raising our sons. Once I told a family at a restaurant that I loved their country, that its people were beautiful.

"Shame on you," the young man reprimanded me.

Had my wits been about me, I could have responded with more than a laugh. "Believe me," I could have told him, "I have my days." I have days when Amman's grinding traffic shreds my nerves, when the city's disorganization slaps me awake and I lament its lack of green spaces. I've stood on my apartment rooftop, looking east toward Iraq, and stared this colorless city in the face: cinderblock buildings sprouting satellite dishes and water tanks, some faced with chiseled stone, others with stucco, everything cubic and sun-dried.

I've lived through storms when the world turns orange with dust, when I've closed the windows and still smelled powdery silt creeping in, clogging my sinuses and throat. I've left west

Amman's cosmopolitan enclave and driven north to Mafraq, east to Azraq, south to Ma'an. On these stretches of road, little fills my vision but rocks, dirt, and plastic bags and bottles caught in chain-link fences.

I could have told that young man how I get irked by nosy, interfering people who tell me how I should raise my sons. How I hate when drivers fling trash from their car windows. How people smoke more per capita than any other country in the world. How I can recognize men and women who care more about outward appearances than inner honesty, who flatter rather than speak truth.

I also could have told him, "I understand." I know unemployment hovers close to 25 percent. I know freedom of expression is limited, water is scarce, and schools are overcrowded. I know foreign aid never seems to trickle down to ordinary people, that many cheat and lie and use family connections to get positions they don't deserve. I see the flaws in this place, the brokenness.

But I've had more than a decade of practice seeing beyond grating superficialities to deeper realities—and beyond those, to the beauty and potential in every place and person. Before our first anniversary, Austin and I moved to Israel for two years of study and work. There we experienced the joys and tensions of living in a land God calls the apple of his eye. Then in 2015, we moved to the Hashemite Kingdom of Jordan—a ragged polygon of mostly resourceless land, a nation that emerged from the dust of the Ottoman Empire. Here I really began to search for beauty deeper than what meets the eye. Call me a mystic, "a kid finding kingdom in the ash heap," as Jessie van Eerden defines the term. Maybe that's who I am: a person who believes God visits.

Looking at the colchicum, I see more than flowers—I see their promise. They are fragile yet visible proof, a temporal, fleeting fulfillment of Isaiah's words: *The desert will bloom.* Isaiah not only refers to literal plants and deserts, of course. Flowers are metaphors that can give rise to a thousand imaginings.

In his prophecy, Isaiah sketches the possibilities he envisions: sight in place of blindness, songs of praise in exchange for muteness, pools springing from the burning ground. Instead of sighs of sorrow, he sees people rejoicing. He paints the future restoration of a geographical area, where processions of singing people will enter Jerusalem—that epicenter of redemption all the prophets saw, that place to which the collective eyes of this region are constantly turned. What could these metaphors, in all their fullness, mean for the Middle East today? If colchicum can resurrect from papery, dead-looking corms, why not these places? Why not us?

Some consider faith an old-fashioned way of understanding the world. Some call those who are assured of unseen things deluded. But let's imagine that these promises and prophecies are real and trustworthy. What if we consider belief our work and faith our most essential and necessary task? And what if, as a result of believing, we begin to see the glory of God infusing every little thing?

I like the words of Liang Dan-Fong, a Chinese-born painter who visited Jordan in the late 1970s. Her artwork depicting tourist locations such as Jerash, Petra, and Wadi Rum has a light touch. In the prologue to her published collection of watercolors, she writes of an Eastern mindset she recognized in Jordan because of her own Oriental background. "In countries where natural resources are in short and favourable conditions often rare, it is especially necessary to employ a total will-power in achieving spiritual civilization."

Spiritual civilization. Is that what we can name the invisible scaffolding I also recognize in this place? To my Western ears, faith is manifest here in such direct, plain language. Every conversation, every social interaction is laced with references to God. Even at traffic lights, I read calligraphied signs that implore me to remember him. Driving north out of Amman, past one of the region's largest Palestinian refugee camps, green placards strapped to fence posts declare his names: the Glorious, the Merciful, the Holy, the Creator, the Forgiver. Everywhere I find God calling. Everywhere he reminds me to believe.

When I activate my faith, the world ignites. Belief wakes me to alternate realities and creates new dimensions. I see staggering potential lodged in a dry bone, a rock, a wasteland. *The desert will bloom*, Isaiah prophesied, and frankly, that's the least of it. The lame will dance. The dead will rise. The blind will see trees walking like men. The minarets will sing praise—endless exaltations to the great indwelling God who has no rival.

What if every speck of beauty in this blasted region was God-placed bait in a dragnet leading to glory? What if every grace was a portent, a reminder that redemption is coming? Like a magpie, I search for signs of him everywhere. Like a treasure hunter, I comb an ancient site for coins. In physical objects—a pomegranate bursting with a thousand miracles, the turquoise flash of a sunbird on an almond tree, careful stitches on flax-colored cloth, olives and bread springing from the ground—I find evidence of him. When I view tangible objects this way, the weight of glory lies heavy.

I believe God's words—that humans are dust made in his image—and so I see his fingerprints on every person I meet. The man wearing a checkered *shemagh,* who's missing half a finger and half his teeth, hands me a paper cup of steaming tea, mirroring God's boundless hospitality. The head-scarfed woman standing in a doorway, waiting, is a picture of the One who waits for me. The young guys showering candy and smiles on my kids point me to the lavish love of heaven. Even raucous neighborhood parties—with drums, bagpipes, and call-and-response songs blasted over megaphones—foreshadow the grandest celebration to come. I believe and see God in these faces, and I pray for the faith to see him in trauma-marked places too—in prisons and refugee camps, in the eyes of the poor, in my own mirror.

In this land, belief enables being. I follow scraps of grace from one parched place to the next, repeating what I know to be true, nourishing myself so I don't wither like desert grass. Belief trusses up my inner being like the ties that guide a jasmine's wandering vines. I ask myself, what if God gave us belief so that amidst evil, horror, and despair, we could perceive love-pierced holes in the darkness and reach out for light, no matter how distant? What if he gave us faith to enable us to stand, so we wouldn't collapse beneath the world's weight, so we could make the impossible real?

On the far side of the Jordan River, I stood on a hillside full of weeds and thorns and colchicum, their opalescent petals like fallen stars. I faced Jerusalem, that potent symbol of hope. My eyes tried to penetrate the haze between me and the other side. As they did, the dry ground rumbled beneath me, a thousand corms erupting beneath my feet.

PART 1

Initiation

CHAPTER 1

Bismillah

Muslims say it as they wash before prayer and before opening the gold-scrolled holy book: *bismillah,* in the name of God, and they murmur it at other predictable moments too, like when entering a mosque or sacrificing a sheep: bismillah, in the name of God, the merciful, the compassionate—and I've heard this invocation on a hundred other occasions: bismillah as my hairdresser makes her first snip, bismillah when a cook flips a pot of rice, bismillah when our milkman dips his can, when my taxi driver tilts over a steep hill, when a workman hoists a refrigerator to his back—everywhere, from every mouth, bismillah summoning blessings, from kids dragging bread through hummus and mothers lifting babies to their breasts and nurses threading needles beneath swabbed skin, bismillah whispered as habit or bismillah as superstitious compulsion, but what I want to know is whether every moment *can* in fact be consecrated, if every act *can* be dedicated to God, and so what if I put it here—bismillah—as Muslims might at the beginning of books, and what if this is my invitation, O LORD, merciful and gracious, slow to anger and abounding in love, my invitation for you to accept the gift of these words written in your name—bismillah—and more than that, a request for you to take me too: to captivate me with a whisper of your name, to engulf me in the embrace of your all-consuming name, to cleave me open and make my soul bloom with clouds of jasmine like incense beckoning and streams of sunbirds like sapphires flashing and everything within me ululating acclaim to your name, singing bismillah while I'm whirling and whirling, ouds strumming and breathy flutes trilling in your name, feet stomping and hands drumming in your name, and me dancing until I'm spilled out in your name like nard anointing your feet and perfuming your name—all of me a prayer, a willing sacrifice, a jubilant river of praise.

CHAPTER 2

Tell Me a Better Way

Winter break of my sophomore year in college, I spent hours with a bundle of colored pencils and an atlas of east-oriented maps of the Holy Land. I labored over this assignment, meant to familiarize me with the Levant and prepare me for a semester in Israel with thirty-nine other students. By focusing on geographical details in swaths of the Old Testament, I was supposed to gain a basic knowledge of a land I had not yet seen. I sat at my parents' kitchen counter, boxing cities in one color, highlighting ancient Israelite paths of pilgrimage and wandering, and tracing routes of attack and retreat until I started seeing them in my hometown's cracked parking lots.

"Make sure you fall in a wadi!" my roommate Kat teased me before I left California, envisioning that if I did, in fact, tumble into a dry riverbed over there, I'd be gallantly rescued by some guy who'd become my husband. That's how the joke went, at least. I was nineteen, a communication major, and not planning to get married. One of those nights after marking my maps, I even sat with my mom near the wood-burning stove and told her I didn't think I'd ever marry, so consumed was I with the idea of pursuing God.

When our United Airlines flight landed in that milk-and-honey land on January 22, 2006—a day that set my life's trajectory—we stepped into the maps we'd been coloring, stepped into a land of brooks and streams, of pomegranates, figs, and vines (and rocks—why did Moses fail to mention the rocks?). This was a land God cared for and kept his eye on day and night. I read those words in the jet-lagged dark of my bunk, suspended above loquacious Heather, who chewed gum continuously and wore her curly hair in pigtails, and cross-country running Melyndee, who hit snooze half a dozen times before inking verses on her forearms and going for miles-long runs at dawn.

I noted this promise about God's care for this place, then emailed it to my parents as proof that I would be safe in the Middle East—even though Hamas had just won elections in Gaza; though a family friend had recently speculated that perhaps Ariel Sharon, comatose after a stroke, was the beast of the apocalypse; though the words *Israel* and *safe* rarely appeared together in news media.

Immediately after stepping off the plane, as our tour bus roared up Highway 1 toward Jerusalem, we began to see Bible stories flashing by our windows in 3D. Todd, the deadpan professor who picked us up from the airport, sat in the guide's seat of the bus and narrated as we drove. "This is a place of testing," he told us. He knew—a father of four, half a world away from family, fresh from the funeral of a young friend. He was reflecting, contemplating out loud to this group of college students buzzed on travel and independence—warning us, if we had ears to hear.

I doubt we heard at first, so exhilarated were we by tromping and traipsing around that land from Dan to Be'er-Sheva. We tumbled out of the bus and followed our tall professor Bill up too many dusty, partially excavated tells to name: Gezer with its hair-dryer wind, Beth Shemesh with a donkey's jawbone hidden in the weeds, Lachish with an Assyrian siege ramp still intact, Megiddo with its armies of millipedes, Beit She'an with its public bathhouse and red clay pipes. We slithered through the Bar Kochva caves like Jewish zealots, through tunnels that gave me years of claustrophobic dreams. We bumbled down the muddy, bamboo-clogged Jordan River in inflatable tubes and biked thirty-three miles around the Sea of Galilee just to say we did. We reenacted battles and gladiator games. We took too many photos and talked too loudly. We cheered like kindergarteners when librarian Becky's marvelous—yea verily, miraculous—treats appeared. (Where in that holy land did she find M&M's and marshmallows?)

Let me ask you: Is there a better way to learn a land than this—by tramping and trailing, wandering and frolicking, wearing your hiking sandals until their soles split halfway up a mountain and all you have is medical tape to bind them? Tell me a better way to join a story than by being grafted in with the dust and illegally picked wildflowers taped in your journal, than by digging out the history yourself in a muddy excavation tunnel, than by sitting under a bush in the wilderness of Paran while grit fills the pages of Deuteronomy and you will the hot sun to burn all these places on your brain. *Remember, remember. Remember the LORD your God and do not forget him.*

* * *

On a ridge in the wilderness of Tekoa, we read about Jehoshaphat, how he was approached in battle by the Ammonites, Moabites, and Edomites, those troublemakers beyond the Jordan. He placed the temple singers in front of his army, and they sang *Hodu l'adonai ki tov, ki leolam chasdo,* just as Bill had taught us on our very first night in Israel. We sang the simple chorus after every field trip, returning bone-tired on the bus with the sun setting over that strip of land so narrow you could practically reach from the river to the sea and roll it up. *Give thanks to the LORD, for he is good.* Praise had defeated Israel's enemies—no swords required, no strategies, just song in the face of battle.

One month into my semester abroad, I needed some praise in a battle, for I felt myself besieged by emerging feelings that contradicted the declaration made to my mom weeks before. This guy who was my friend—tall, quirky, always wearing cargo pants, with blue, blue eyes behind his glasses—when he bandaged the sore feet of a fellow student on a hike, an unexpected seed lodged in my heart. Twelve of us had rented a van to hike to Nahal David, a river-cut canyon near the Dead Sea. We arrived on the sea's shoreline with a couple of tents and a pile of food pillaged from our cafeteria, then camped on a rocky ridge. In the morning we hiked past salt pits near the water's edge, tasting the mineral-rich sand. We arrived at Nahal David, where we splashed in the falls among bamboo and pudgy rock badgers, and all the while, I felt this seed taking root.

A few weeks later, when the whole lot of us camped on a beach beside the Dead Sea, I realized that this guy, Austin, a true friend of mine, might be more than a friend. A struggle ensued between my tender, womanly self who recognized a good man, a kind and humble man—a man who, following a study-abroad program tradition, had given me the literal cake on his twenty-first birthday—and my stubborn self who could not conceive of entertaining a romantic interest *and* devoting myself to God.

Tell me, is love for God supposed to obliterate all other attachments and desires? The psalmist wrote, "Whom have I in heaven but you? And there is nothing on earth that I desire besides you." I wanted to live out the singlemindedness of those words, but with this budding interest, I felt opposed to God. While scrambling up Nahal Arugot after our professor Todd, I tried not to fall in the wadi after the skittering rocks.

By the end of the semester, I'd hashed out my blossoming emotions with God, realized that though unanticipated, they were natural. I spent weeks hiding in God, waiting. Maybe Austin didn't feel the same for me. Maybe he just wanted to graduate and move on with his life. One afternoon while I was writing a research paper in the library, a tiny wad of paper sailed onto my lap. *I need to have an important conversation with you*, it read, Austin's close handwriting in all caps. *Are you free after tonight's lecture?* My heart seized, looking at his back in an orange fleece, hunched over a book. I wrote *yes* and threw the paper back.

A few days later, we took our first picture together in Nahal Parat. Our hair was wet because we'd just stood under a waterfall. My sleeves were rolled up, exposing bare shoulders, and Austin had a clean-shaven, cleft chin. We sat with our arms hugging our knees, a bit of space between us. I pinched myself to make sure it was real. Todd had known, he told everyone in our final chapel meeting. He had seen straight through my attempts at concealment, through Austin's hesitation to declare anything. "I regret that I wasn't the one to get Heather and Austin together," he said with a wry smile. Everyone whooped, and I hid my blushing face.

Before we returned to California, all forty of us gathered on the asphalt near the village's recycling bins and flimsy wooden post office and danced the *hora* under the street lights. I wore a purple, wrap-around skirt I'd bought in Mahane Yehuda and a silver ring made in the Old City of Jerusalem, one that would encircle my thumb for years. *YHWH tov*, it read in punched-out Hebrew letters. *The LORD is good.*

I had passed through a test of emotions and hidden in his refuge, and as I danced jubilantly, I felt like he had rewarded me. Tell me a better way to experience his goodness than by having your consciousness cracked open, revealing that love is not scarce but abundant, that it does not divide but multiplies like loaves and fish. Tell me how else to glimpse the truth that love for God does not obliterate all other loves but rather grounds them, becomes the soil from which all passions spring.

As I danced as part of the hora's inner circle, heart pounding, I felt aware of him watching me.

* * *

Three years later, I became most blessed among women, for I married Austin and returned to Israel and got the job chasing students for not one but two years—seasons in which I lived in crew neck T-shirts, cargo shorts, and hiking sandals. I still wore that ring, a promise to remember: *He is good, he is good, he is good.* My former guides became my colleagues: Becky, the ruddy-faced librarian from a Pennsylvania farm who laughed heartily, wore shirts tucked into denim skirts, and came to our weekly staff meetings with a clipboard of lists and calendars that put my disorganized notes to shame. Benj, a recent PhD graduate with impossibly long legs who was raised in France, disliked butter, and married an Israeli after university. (I may have once argued with him that Nutella is not, in fact, healthy, even though it contains hazelnuts.) He continually suggested innovative ideas to Bill, who was nearly old enough to be my and Benj's dad and had helped found the study-abroad program, and good-naturedly, realistically, shot most of those innovative ideas down.

Austin and I lived in a one-room flat on the moshav where the study-abroad program was based. Yad HaShmona was a communal village of fewer than 200 residents, established by Finnish immigrants in memory of eight Jews whom their government had surrendered to the Nazis during the Holocaust. A jacaranda tree graced our yard, as well as occasional peacocks.

In the evenings, when Austin returned from the university in Jerusalem where he was studying for a master's degree in ancient Near Eastern history, we hosted college students, feeding them Middle Eastern tacos (our California roots laid bare), spicy meat and cheese stuffed in pita bread. We celebrated the cycles of

Jewish holidays, setting up Passover feasts, building sukkahs, fasting and praying on Yom Kippur after taking pictures in the middle of the empty freeway, lighting candles and eating jelly donuts during Hanukkah. On Holocaust Remembrance Day, we stopped and stood with millions of Israelis while the bomb sirens pierced and wailed.

We kept hiking, of course. In Nahal Yehudiyah, spring steamed like the jungle. There was so much dew that a student in a wife-beater and head cloth shouted, "Them flowers is bling-blingin'!" In Nahal Ammud during Passover, we said "*Chag sameach!*" to every Israeli we passed on the thistle-crowded path, then pitched our tent in a field, waking in the middle of the night giggling because Austin feared the cows would eat his wallet. After evenings galloping on marl cliffs like the moon, we climbed Masada, that wilderness fortress built by King Herod and used as a hideout during the Jewish Revolt. After hiking up with students, I perched overlooking the Dead Sea and Jordan, where those pesky enemies of Israel had lived, then wandered to admire the frescoes still bright after centuries.

There was so much good—that's the bottom line—and God was so good, like my ring kept reminding me and the Bible studies in the bomb shelter with college girls—earnest-faced and open—and the worship songs in the *kehilah* surrounded by people from every nation, tribe, and tongue. There wasn't a better way to learn about the LORD, the God of Abraham, Isaac, and Jacob, than by living in this place where he had moved and worked, was there? Surely some people back home thought that—a little envious that we had this opportunity to live in the land of the Bible for two years.

I was living this reality, though it included all the mundanities no one back home envisioned: the pell-mell parking lots, terrifying visa renewals at the Ministry of the Interior, my failed kitchen garden. Surrounded by so many literal wildernesses—Judea, Paran, Zin, Sinai—I often reflected on the warning our professors had spoken multiple times: *This is a place of testing.* I wondered not if but when testing would come for me.

* * *

One day on our bus ride home from Tekoa, all was surrounded by golden halos—the groves of gray-green olive trees, the limestone bedrock protruding from the soil like a backbone through the low-slung hills of the West Bank. I spotted two guys on the side of the road, their arms pulled back. Rocks hit the windows of the bus, shattering the glass; fine shards sprayed over our ducked heads. The students seemed unhurt, but when Benj stood up and turned to look at us, his face was bleeding where a baseball-sized rock had hit him on the right cheekbone. Our bus driver, Issa, continued to drive as he and Benj called the police and cool air poured in where the rocks had come through. Every now and then, chunks of glass fell from the bus door like ice from a melting floe.

While Austin answered questions from the shocked students ("What just happened? Why? Who were those guys?"), I wondered how Issa felt, having the windows of his bus wrecked by angry teenagers, Palestinians like himself. How did he feel about us? Presumably, we were pro-Zionist tourists who were not welcome and who had just become targets. And what about his bus, now collateral in a conflict that, to me, was no longer black-and-white but more and more gray.

As we parted ways at the moshav, Austin told Issa we were sorry about his bus. He responded in Hebrew, "I am glad it was the windows, not a life."

Another day, in the middle of a field trip, we heard on the radio that a bus stop near Jerusalem's Central Bus Station had been bombed. Austin frequented this stop four or five times a week. Around thirty people were wounded by the four-and-a-half-pound bomb that had been hidden in a duffel bag on the sidewalk. One person died, a fifty-five-year-old Scottish woman named Mary. She was soft-spoken, had strawberry blonde down on her face. I know because I knew her, had been neighbors with her for a while, had prayed with her in the same congregation.

While the students scattered in Netanya to find pizza, Becky and I walked on the beach, reeling. In the days that followed, surrounded by skittish Israelis, I wondered at the irony. They knew Mary's name from the news reports, but I, a foreigner, *knew* her, also a stranger in this strange land. Tell me how you'd feel in this situation. Wouldn't you reason that this trial had been fashioned specifically for you? Wouldn't you feel rattled, start to question the intentions of a good God toward you?

At a shelter in the armpit of Tel Aviv, an American named Dave looked at me and said, "Are you sure you know what you're getting into?" Before moving to Israel, I'd been stricken by stories of women trafficked into sex work. The Door of Hope was a place I could serve some of these women, a safe house where prostitutes struggling with drug addiction congregated when they weren't finding clients. The day we met, Dave saw through me, assessed me correctly—a small-town girl who hadn't seen the horrors I was about to see week after week as I took the bus from Yad HaShmona to the city to volunteer there.

I saw women sitting at the food counter, haunted, their limbs like chicken bones, their legs rotting from the drug-induced euphoria of scratching. We'd serve them Nescafé in paper cups and pasta alongside Dave's confetti coleslaw, then wash the dishes with an eye on the shower to make sure no one shot up in there. We'd sweep up rat droppings and launder mounds of clothes covered with hovering flies and jeans that smelled like semen, then pray in that basement that smelled like damp mold and bleach—never simple prayers, but battling, war-like prayers, ones that ached for the Messiah with fragile, gritty hope. We saw visions of restoration, of the racing, pure blue spirit of God falling from heaven, declaring prisoners free and releasing captives from their chains.

Griefs compounded. In the United States, my aunt died, and Hilkka, one of the moshav's founders, died. We lined up on the side of the hill and took turns shoveling dirt onto Hilkka's coffin, a plywood box draped with an Israeli flag. Persistent illnesses crippled me: urinary tract and yeast infections, strep throat, pink eye, stomach ailments. I struggled to communicate with the Israeli doctors at the urgent care. One day, a taxi driver asked Austin and me why we didn't have kids yet after two years of marriage. "Some Orthodox Jews have four kids in three years!" he bellowed, heaping shame on me as if part of me didn't work.

Once Austin leaned on the kitchen counter and told me about his class with a liberal Jewish scholar. He felt shaken by theories that put doubt on traditional views of the Bible's composition and historicity. His tremor felt like a microcosm of mine, a tiny spike on my Richter scale that was quivering, trembling uncontrollably. I'd been writing in my journal for weeks, praying. "Is my belief system a web I've constructed around myself for protection, insulation from reality? If I broke out, would I find the world beyond me entirely different than how I perceive it now? How do I know my core beliefs aren't manmade principles fabricated to explain the world? Is all this suffering going to be worth it, or am I just deluding myself, inventing a purpose for life because I need hope?"

I twisted the ring on my thumb, thought of how God's steadfast love was supposed to endure forever. This was the one thing I had always known. But my suffering, my exposure to evil, was adding up, and I wasn't confident anymore. Tell me how God could be good and allow all this crap to exist. That's what I needed to know.

I felt a magnificent crackling of doubts and rage erupt through me like lightning. I sensed a great tearing of the blanket I'd stitched around myself. My soul looked out, terrified, as questions swamped me, as I considered whether to step away from the security of answers I'd believed all my life. Anything could buckle and crack under the weight of those doubts. I felt I had two choices: leave what I had always believed, casting it aside as some false support to help people through life, or cling to God and trust him, although I didn't understand him. I considered oblivion, annihilation, the idea that perhaps he was invented. I felt an icy, cobalt bar of fear in my spine that sucked my breath away.

* * *

Around this time, I hiked from Jericho to Jerusalem—fifteen miles into the sun-saturated wilderness, an ascent of 3,500 feet, a path from the lowest city on earth to the city of God. As I set off with Bill and the college students, we scanned the ruins of a Herodian palace overlooking the modern city of Jericho, where a Palestinian flag flew over an unfinished concrete building. A few miles into our walk, we sighted the bubbly, turquoise domes of a monastery built into the wall of Wadi Qilt.

Eventually our path wound past a Bedouin family's shelter—scrap wood, blankets, corrugated metal—where Bill chatted with a few kids in basic Arabic. They munched crackers and stared at him, frizzy-haired, wearing dirty pullover sweatshirts. Their mother emerged from the doorway of their home carrying a saucepan full of green pears. Her smile beamed like the rhinestones on her black hijab.

We treaded a windy ridge opposite Ma'ale Adummim, one of the largest Israeli settlements in the West Bank. The Mount of Olives sat ahead of us, its three towers rising toward smeared cumulus clouds. Wan light put crisp definition on everything—fine winter grass, the rutted stones of a Roman road, yellow starburst flowers and inch-tall irises pushing out of the packed soil. Bottlebrush caterpillars crawled out of glistening webs fastened to rocks and plants, emerging into the wide world.

On field trips like these, I usually had work responsibilities, like photographing the students for the website or literally coming into step with young people who felt discouraged, homesick, or weary. But that day, on a bonus weekend trip, I allowed myself to participate instead of mentor. I soaked in the route that ancient Jews walked when coming from Galilee to

Jerusalem for annual festivals, absorbed the setting of the Good Samaritan parable while putting one foot in front of another on the path where it was imagined. Tell me a better way than this, a better way to commit to memory the stories you've heard all your life.

God knew I needed a mental break too, a day disengaged from the agitation brewing in my soul. And though doubts chattered around my edges, frittering the placid security I had long enjoyed, I was barely aware of how the wilderness landscape I walked through symbolized what was about to occur inside me. I didn't realize that my interior, so long a place of abundance, was about to be stripped.

For years, that hike acted as a keystone in my memory, occupying a disproportionate amount of space in my mind. On the day of the trek, I did not attribute any significance to it, aside from it being the longest hike I'd taken in Israel. An incoming tide of doubt was licking my feet, but for years I mostly recalled visual details I recorded on my blog: Issawiya, a Palestinian neighborhood that sits west of Israel's security wall, bisected by a road clogged with puddles and bounded by grass and trash. A used car lot, concrete buildings tattooed with Arabic graffiti, a guy who threw stones at us, a flock of milk-white herons rising. I couldn't perceive the meaning in these contrasting images— the poverty and hostility witnessed in Issawiya contra the quiet wilderness we'd passed through—couldn't ascertain why they left such an imprint on me.

More than a decade later, I can see how this journey foreshadowed aspects of who I would become. Strands of my future were lifted like warp threads in a rug, hinting at the pattern that would later emerge. I recognize an interest in Arabic, a desire to connect with misunderstood peoples of the desert, an emerging ability to find nourishing grace in unexpected, blank places. But 2011 was too early, I guess, too early to grasp how the road through the wilderness symbolized bigger realities, how it could act as a metaphor for life with its ascent to glory through inevitable suffering. On that day, the basics had not even solidified in my head; that was day one of bootcamp.

"Faith isn't about being right or having all the answers or avoiding pain," I read in a magazine article by Rachel Held Evans. "It's about refusing to give up when it seems like you should." I tucked the article in my journal—a notebook I'd decorated collage-style with the Arabic alphabet, my favorite chai tea label in Hebrew, a handwritten Psalm about Jerusalem given to me by Bill's wife.

Were the doubts and questions I faced natural for a young person who'd had a safe, happy childhood? Was it normal for a person largely unfamiliar with sorrow, unacquainted with grief, to need principles of suffering clarified, sharpened? I was comforted by the presence of a fellow pilgrim on my tumultuous path. "Take it from me," Evans concluded with epistle-like brevity. "Faith is resilient. Doubt is surmountable. God is good. I know, because my faith shouldn't be alive . . . but by the grace of God, it survives." I latched onto these few fundamentals like gospel.

We returned to the U.S. several months later so Austin could begin a PhD program in Old Testament in the Chicago suburbs. We settled into a refugee housing complex, a place where I realized I'd resolved so little in my struggle with doubt, a place where I was confronted with my rawest misgivings about God.

Dave sent a letter from Tel Aviv; one of the prostitutes I'd known, a Russian woman with a swastika tattooed on her shoulder, had died. Wah Wah, a Burmese neighbor with an autistic son, was being abused by her husband. A little boy got run over by a car in the parking lot. A three-year-old named April Paw died of a heart infection. Where was God, and if he really cared, then why, why, why?

* * *

I asked Austin recently while driving to the grocery store in Amman, "What did I learn in that season in Israel?" He focused ahead, navigating our sedan through bonkers traffic. He still has the bluest eyes. His hair is now evenly salt-and-pepper on top, prematurely grayed by his doctoral program, caring for me in a season of mental unwellness, raising two active boys, and teaching graduate-level courses in Arabic.

"I don't think that crisis had any bright resolutions," he replied.

I agreed—and yet I also knew one thing: My understanding of God deepened, diversified in the eye of that hurricane. During my semester in Israel as a nineteen-year-old, I'd been so focused on God's goodness that I neglected other aspects of his character. Unconsciously, I'd held the assumption that if God was good, that meant he was nice—that shallow, insipid word we use with kids. I didn't want a nice God, I realized. And I didn't have one—that he had taught me clearly.

As I struggled with God honestly in Israel and afterward, I found that he was indescribably good—a descriptor including awe-inspiring, majestic, jealous, just, and righteous—a God I could not comprehend, one who could not be contained by paltry English words. Was I willing to live with the mystery of him, the impossibility of reconciling him with the wrecked world around me? Did suffering and evil negate his love and presence, or was it my deceptive heart fooling me, my fickle emotions and ever-changing circumstances clouding my view of him?

I asked these questions in my journals, in less-clear terms, and in my mind on long bus rides and while hiking or grading papers. On Shabbat afternoons when the students roamed Jerusalem, I hid on the swing beneath our neighbor's building, obscured by ivy, and wrestled with God, assimilating experience with truth, discarding some half-truths and weaving others into my expanding view of reality.

I wanted someone to tell me if I'd survive my first, frightening foray into spiritual wilderness. I sensed I needed to learn to hold contradictions in silence, but I didn't have many examples or much experience with that idea. Would I be able to become a sort of mystic—definitely an unfamiliar word in my evangelical tradition—embracing awe and wonder, the uncomfortableness of doubt, the tension of existing in liminal places? Would I be able surrender to unknowing, thus being united with someone greater than myself, with the One who built such contradiction into the universe so I would choose creaturely dependence as I ought? Would I learn to rejoice in beauty and truth, and lament evil and wrongdoing, all while knowing one thing—that God would make everything beautiful in its time?

The Jewish prophet Hosea assured me this was possible. In the midst of an admittedly disturbing narrative, he used the image of God calling to his people in the wilderness.

Perhaps because I spent hours with prostitutes every week, Hosea's graphic passages about sexual abuse did not faze me. After walking through Tel Aviv's red-light district, where I was sometimes heckled and mistaken as one of them, I rode the bus home. Driving through the land where God had used flawed judges and wacky prophets to call his people to repentance, these words gripped and nourished me.

> Behold, I will allure her, and bring her
> into the wilderness and speak tenderly to her.
> And there I will give her her vineyards
> and make the Valley of Achor a door of hope.

Violent metaphors aside, I became convinced that Hosea's story was a portrait of God's risk-taking love—and that his love was for me. He wanted me to know him, not just his book or the geography of his land or the history of his people, but *him*. And honestly, tell me—was there a better way to get to know him than by losing my health and loved ones and small measures of security, to then be cradled in the palms of his hands, a warm refuge from storms?

What better way was there to meet this God who engaged himself to me than by letting him lead me into the harsh, bewildering wilderness of reality, where I'd be hedged in, unable to find love or salvation apart from him? What better way than by being called out by his whisper, than by stepping from darkness into marvelous light—the bountiful, shimmering light of his face?

I sat at the kitchen table in our tiny Israeli flat with the sun falling on the wide windowsill, the laundry line outside skirted by leggy rosemary bushes. There I identified with Jacob as he wrestled with the angel of the LORD. I knew the groaning, the twisting of sweaty limbs, the pain of dislocation, the lasting effects of touching God. And as I sat on the cusp of so much more, a lifetime's worth of learning, really, God transfigured before me. He transformed from a simple, smooth stone to a fierce, multi-faceted jewel that fractured and threw wild light a hundred directions—harder to put in my pocket but infinitely more attractive, mystifying, and precious.

CHAPTER 3

Beyond the Jordan

The Prayer Tree

I ought to remember the mosaics, the cornerstone of the church, the hazy view into the Holy Land. But I have seen too many mosaics and limestone walls. What I saw—what I remember—is the oak tree on the eastern edge of the archaeological site. It was a normal oak tree with knobby bark, hardy leaves that look perpetually dusty, a sprinkling of acorns, pollen streamers hanging. Its lower branches, though, were tied up in trash.

Somehow I knew what it was without knowing: a prayer tree. It didn't look holy; it looked dirty. It looked like the Western Wall in Jerusalem, with a wide, greasy stripe where worshipers rest their foreheads, its cracks stuffed with prayer notes in all languages, written on scraps of journal paper, receipts, and gum wrappers. Twice a year they pry the prayers from the wall— 1 million every year—and bury them in the cemetery on the

Mount of Olives. I too have a prayer there, buried somewhere beneath the dirt on the mountain that prophecy says the Messiah will split in two when he returns.

I step closer to look at the tree. I see blue and red ribbons—maybe the people who hung these came with a ready prayer. But it looks like most people were unprepared. The lower branches of the oak are draped in flotsam—the ripped-out seam of a T-shirt, a black plastic bag, dried wet wipes, toilet paper, a strip of rubber, crumpled notebook paper. What kinds of prayers were these, placed by Muslims and Christians alike? Does the wet wipe plead for a baby, the plastic bag for peace? I see Syria in the distance, and Iraq is a day's drive away.

My son, David, tries to climb the sagging rope between the path and the mosaics. I catch him, meander with our friends, try to be interested in the tops of columns and the faint outline of buildings. Mostly, though, I think about prayer trees. I like the idea of hoisting up a prayer and letting it flap before God while I move on. I'm a somewhat agitated woman these days; my attention span is frayed, I distract easily. Sometimes I feel like a pile of electrical wires smoking and sparking on the ground. Prayer without ceasing, but without the labor—that sounds attractive.

Once I stood in Jerusalem's Church of the Holy Sepulchre, the most holy site in Christendom, mesmerized by a row of burning tapers. Candles in churches—that's the same idea as prayer trees, right? Wax crusted the edge of the sandbox in which they were planted. I was transfixed, staring at the candles as pilgrims and tourists milled around me.

Suddenly a priest approached, gathered the candles in his hand, and blew them out. Their wicks smoldered, and curls of white smoke rose toward the light sifting down from the domed ceiling. I felt stunned. Could he really just blow out those candles? People paid for those and prayed for those! What did putting them out mean? Seven years later, that memory still runs in my mind, untethered, the questions begging answers.

I am like the disciples of Christ. "Teach us to pray," they said, even though they'd heard him teach month after month, probably heard him pray hundreds of times. How many times have I prayed these four words recently? Enveloped in a fog of anxiety and exhaustion, the monotony of washing clothes and wrangling a toddler, the uncomfortable nature of a new culture, language, and place, I have been reduced to this little sentence: "Teach me to pray."

Leaving the archaeological site, I want a prayer tree. Those branches are stronger than my arms and can hold for decades. I'm like the prophet Moses—just a mortal. Not far from here, in the Sinai desert, he needed Aaron and Hur to hold up his arms as his muscles grew weary. I need someone, something, to hold me up, one on the right hand and one on the left, if the battle within me is going to be won.

Kite Flying

It was definitely *not* love at first sight. As we drove by fluorescent-lit vegetable stands and stone buildings on the way from the airport, I thought, *Here we go again.* Every detail resembled life on the western side of the river: the press-button light switches; the cold, salmon- and beige-flecked floors; the storm shutters lowered over windows as snow fell from a curdled sky. It was not love at first week or even first month.

Something changed on a spring night while I sipped tea on a balcony overlooking Amman. Austin and I sat above the car exhaust-darkened buildings of downtown—*al-balad*—packed together and street-threaded like a pinball game, the people and cars silver beads inside. Above this rose a scrappy green hill called the Citadel, where several pillars from a Roman temple stand near the restored dome of an Umayyad-era palace. Four thousand years ago, this was the capital of the Ammonites. Two thousand years ago, it was called Philadelphia. Now it is the heart of Jordan's capital.

I saw a flock of pigeons flying in loops and figure eights, dark until they reached the zenith of their climb, then bright as their underwings flashed in a dive. They responded to high-pitched whistles from a man on his apartment rooftop. Arab men love raising pigeons and doves. It's a hobby for many, who keep them in cages and fly them at dusk. Multiple flocks were visible now, each dipping, soaring, and weaving to its owner's call.

Then I noticed the kites. They were like stars; I saw one and then another, and the deeper I looked, the more I perceived. I knew kites were important in Asia but had yet to learn their significance in the Arab world. I didn't know that the children of Gaza held the Guinness record for the most kites flown at once—thousands of homemade kites flown by thousands of children living under a blockade. Because of travel restrictions, a Guinness official was unable to attend the event in July 2011, but United Nations employees verified that more than 13,000 kites flew that day, enough to break the world record held by China.

Something about flying a kite brings freedom to the soul. The fine string between your fingers sets your sights on things above. Earthly cares dissolve—burdens like blockades, the lack of electricity and medical supplies and materials to rebuild your bombed-out house. Difficulties like tense relationships, miscommunications, and regional unrest.

Two months before we sat overlooking the balad, King Abdullah had addressed the nation, responding to an Islamic State video of a Jordanian fighter pilot burned alive in a cage. "Raise your head," he told his people in the face of terror's cinching noose. "You are Jordanian." People had painted those phrases on white fabric, mounted them over streets, and posted them in traffic circles. For days, those banners flew over streams of cars and pedestrians like oversized kites. I stopped in the street once or twice to sound out the big cursive letters. I tucked the quietly defiant words in my heart.

I now could see dozens of kites rising in the dusky sky, soaring above still nameless-to-me neighborhoods. They tugged on their strings, guided by taxi drivers, teachers, and falafel makers, rising above pollution and traffic and poverty to fly.

Though I still understood so little, my heart lifted with them.

A Boy Named Peace

They were Palestinians. When their first son was born and they wanted to name him Gandhi, Hamas, the political authority in the Gaza Strip, told them, "You can't call him that. It's not a Muslim name." But the boy's father admired that man of peace and was determined. Eventually, he got his way.

Gandhi's mother told me this story the first day I visited her, while we cooked and I learned some of my first Arabic words. *Basal*, onion. *Bandora*, tomato. *Batata*, potato. The family fled

Gaza for Gandhi's sake in July 2014, when Israel was bombing in response to salvos of Hamas-fired rockets. After arriving in Jordan, the toddler spent two weeks in the hospital, shattered by psychological trauma.

We sat on the marble porch step drinking hot, sugared chamomile tea, which she served on a silver tray. I wore her slippers and burned my tongue. *Sukhun.* Hot. She knew some people here in Amman, she said, but felt she was still "living in the war." We watched our boys play in the slanted sunshine, did our best to break up fights between kids without a common language.

One week later, she called me. "We have to go back to Gaza," she said. "The *mukhabarat* won't let us stay." Though both parents had secured jobs in Amman, the Jordanian intelligence department denied them refugee status and directed them to leave the next time the border crossing opened between Egypt and Gaza.

She told me how they had applied for refugee status in the United States and been denied. What can you do when you sign your name, swearing truthfulness, and the truth you must write is this: Religion: Muslim. Place of Residence: the Gaza Strip.

Before she left, the mother of Gandhi gave me a keychain shaped like Palestine, overlaid with the colors of the Palestinian flag. Welded beside it stood the figure of a boy. He was barefoot and wearing patched clothes, his hands crossed behind his back. *Handala* is his name—same as a bitter melon that grows in desert soils and determinedly returns even when chopped down. "This boy is the symbol of our struggle for justice," she told me.

In Arabic, the word for *strip* comes from the verbal root *to cut*. With this in mind, I think of that little piece of land, cut off from the outside world. When my phone lights up with a text from Gandhi's mother, I am still a little surprised that I know someone there. I look close when I read the news, for although cut off from me now, someone I know lives there. If I'm watchful, I may see a woman walking the rubble-filled streets, holding the hand of a boy named Peace.

Water Day

Really, Jordan is a desert, one of the most water-needy countries in the world. But on Wednesday mornings in our neighborhood, smack in the middle of the city map, you'd think you were in Paradise.

When I step into the street, I smell rain but know it's impossible. Summer has come, and dust storms have blown in from the Sahara or Saudi, leaving everything dull. The big Chinese sumac across the street, the grape arbors in every third neighbor's yard—their leaves pressed out sticky bright two months ago, but now they're dust-covered and weary.

Then I remember. The water "comes" today. Today women stay home to do laundry and bathe children. Men bucket-wash their cars and spray down their sidewalks like their sidewalks are lawns. People water nonliving things extravagantly. The muddy run-off pours down the street, kicking up fine powder that puffs like smoke.

I turn north, hopping over wet tire marks that stripe the asphalt. At the corner, our neighbors' Sri Lankan housekeeper splashes water on the porch stairs and squeegees it down with a foamy swish and tap. In front of the electric company, water trickles out of a drainage pipe. I duck under the big leaves of a redbud tree to watch the water on its meandering journey toward the garbage bins at the intersection.

Water wasn't consumed like this on the other side of the river. When we moved into our flat in Israel, our elderly neighbor advised us to keep a bucket in our shower to catch cold water while waiting for the hot to come. We collected it and used it to water the red geraniums in our courtyard.

Jordanian geraniums, unlike their Israeli counterparts, get liberally doused on water day. In many senses, Arabs let one of their proverbs guide them: "The greatest crime is finding water in the desert and not sharing it." Though the system forces Jordanians to conserve—you only get what goes into your storage tank once a week—most really have no sense of conservation. They are wildly generous in all things. Even during Ramadan, when they fast all day from food and drink, they make up for it at night with feasts.

During the first Ramadan we experienced in Jordan—those thirty days of fasting—Austin, David, and I took walks at sunset. The streets were deserted, and all we could hear was the sound of dishes and silverware clattering as families broke their fasts. A few people still walking home would stop in the street to open bottles of water, quenching day-long desire. Although I hadn't been fasting, I felt their relief.

At the same time, on an incorporeal level, I didn't feel relieved. Months later, I'm still not satisfied. Water and food can't push back the wasteland fluttering on the edge of myself—a dry, anxiety-pitted place I've visited before. All this water around me, streaming unhindered down the street and splitting the dust before it, reminds me of how the wilderness withers and burns. I sense it threatening the vulnerable borders of my soul.

An ancient poet, well-acquainted with both literal and psychological deserts, wrote a love song to his Creator: "As the deer pants for the water brooks, so my soul pants for you, O God." How is it we can thirst for something intangible and unseen, something that cannot go down our throats? What makes our invisible souls parch and crack like puzzles, robbing us of any ability to soak up life? How do we find streams to revive us, rivers that flow through Paradise?

I imagine myself a traveler on the edge of a desert. My head throbs a little; my body aches from dehydration. Before me stretches a shimmering distance. Who knows if what I see is a true oasis or only a mirage?

As I squint into the stinging sand, I smell water. And I wonder, *Must that desert really be mine?*

Al-Fajr

Every morning, I jolt awake to the morning call to prayer. *Al-fajr*, they call it, the dawn. With the mosque just four buildings away, the sound breaks through shuttered windows, closed doors, white noise, and earplugs like a radio turned on mid-song. Chanted Arabic pierces the air, emanating from minarets ringed with green fluorescent lights, casting a web over this city of millions. Sometimes notes seem inverted, skewed from their daytime sounds. Sometimes I can distinguish words; once I woke up and thought I heard angels.

This morning I hear rain. Its soft pattering invades my dreams, and it takes time to sort out what's what. That's wind slapping the wet awning above the neighbor's car. That's water hitting the tiles of the porch. I relax my braced muscles and listen.

When I was a girl, the rain gutter outside my room gurgled me to sleep beneath my mermaid sheets. A heavy polyester blanket covers me now, on the other side of the world from childhood. Sometimes I feel like an old woman, but I'll be just thirty this year, and it's about time. Both experiences and images can make the soul age. Somehow I've seen a lot of both, and here in Jordan I continue to see them.

This week I passed a crowd of women, mostly dressed in long black abayas and headscarves. A storage-shed-turned-copy-center accommodated a swell of people with paperwork, and a man with a pushcart sold sesame baguettes and paper cups of tea. The women were Syrians, I learned. The one I spoke with—I could catch her meaning beneath her accent's mask—she said she walked across the city to wait in this line for aid. She has four children, and her husband is still in Syria. Her hand was bandaged because yesterday a policeman hit her when the crowd became restless.

Another woman like her came to our door recently, asking for rent money and diapers for her baby. As a torrent of blessing-strewn supplications flowed from her mouth, she raised her eyes and lifted her hands. *O God, help me.*

It could be raining in Syria too, we're so close. I think about how close it is, how my friend used to go to Damascus for summer vacation. How my Arabic teacher once answered her phone in the middle of class to hear that her family's home in Aleppo had been bombed. How in Raqqa, the Islamic State's self-proclaimed capital, they behead people and stone women for adultery. Sometimes I lie in bed thinking about how they would kill me, an American infidel, right alongside the covered women.

There are other things I've seen that appear unexpectedly in the night, like ghosts. The dilated pupils of a dead child, the body of a boy run over by a car, rail-thin women selling their bodies in the street, crucified men. Unfortunately, time doesn't heal all wounds. Moving to new countries doesn't wipe your soul shiny clean.

Sometimes, when I can't sleep, I wander out to our enclosed porch. On my knees, I search out the moon, no matter its size, or a star big enough to give light. I rest my chin on the stone windowsill and part the curtains to watch the street. In the building across from ours, rented almost entirely by refugees, a few windows are still lit. Turnover there is rapid; every few months a faded "for rent" sign appears in a window. I'm comforted to know that others are awake.

This morning the rain soothes me drowsy. I think about the coming mosque call, about the words *Allahu akbar*— words stamped on black flags and proclaimed over orange-clad martyrs, but also words that will soon be whispered by mothers and fathers and children on the floors of rented rooms and in tents issued by the UNHCR—the United Nations' refugee agency. *God is great,* they'll pray with the rain, *God is great.*

But God, I'll add, *what in the world are you doing?*

How You Walk

First of all, don't look men in the eyes. Eyes are powerful, you know that, my love? Windows to your soul. You can't use that power in the street. No singing, no laughing. Unless you want to look American—then, by all means, go ahead. But raise your head, girl. You aren't a doormat. You are strong, confident. You must be strong out there.

Always wear long pants and sleeves. Always wear shirts that cover your hips. Don't wear your hair loose or wet, and cover your neck. Shoes? As you like. Watch what other women do and copy them. And wear sunglasses. They're classy, and they hide where your eyes are really looking.

But how do I cover my spirit? How do I protect my soul?

What do you mean, *habeebti*?

There was a man. Up from the convenience store, the one with the kind owner. Down from the electric company where the blind man sells glasses, as if he could give sight. Across from the home of the paralyzed man, spoon-fed on his sun porch. Below the neighbors with canary cages zip-tied to their window bars. The place where Egyptian workers wash cars, where the sidewalks crumble from olive tree roots and cats tear open bags of trash. This man—he touched me and then looked into my eyes. He saw the nakedness of my soul.

Why didn't you hit him? Why didn't you throw your shoe at him? There, there, don't cry. It's not your fault, you didn't do anything wrong. You shouted at him, though? Good. Come, sit here and drink this tea because of your tears.

I feel shot through. I feel every wound I ever had reopening.

I know, dear one. It happens to all of us. I know, that doesn't make it right. Have you heard of Rumi, the poet? "The wound is the place where the light enters you." That's what he wrote. True words, those. No, you can't imagine it now, but listen to me. One day you'll wake up, and the rising sun will shoot you through. It'll eat you up with bright, and nothing will be able to stop you with that glory inside.

Oh, but yes, my love, you can cry now. Right now, everything can be darkness.

Deliver Us from Evil

At the end of our street, Iraqis play backgammon in the park. They gather in clusters—two men straddling the cinderblock wall or the bench under the palm tree, a board between them, other men standing around, all focused on the dice. Midday Friday, when Muslim men stream past them on their way to the mosque, they just keep playing.

As long as the weather is good, they're there. Jobless, they gather to socialize and pass the time while waiting for a visa to Australia, a call from the Canadian embassy, some news about the situation in Mosul or Erbil. Like Jordanians, they wear collared shirts and slacks and carry prayer beads in their pockets. With similar strands, you can say the rosary or remember the ninety-nine names of Allah. Take your pick; the Iraqis already have.

On Thursday nights, the parking lot at church is a mad mess of Iraqis, Egyptians, and Jordanians. We press into the fray— Austin, David, and I—into the melee of hand-shaking and kissing and blessing, into the men with their wives, zigzagged by children playing tag while munching chips, past strollers with fat babies who look like toasted marshmallows in their early spring bundles. The Iraqi accent is everywhere—"eh" instead of "ah" when they agree with each other, verbs conjugated like newscasters and poets.

Middle-aged ladies with dyed and styled hair pull me into hugs and exclaim over my blond child. If only I could remember the names to match these familiar faces. They remember me because I visited them—the little American woman with the Jordanian church members. Visits mean a lot.

The first night I went visiting, I accompanied an elderly Jordanian couple. We lugged in a sack of beans and oil, tea and tomato paste, then sat on the edge of the couch to hear the Iraqi family's story. I strained to catch their words, slippery like fish.

Once we visited an artist who pulled her collection of newsprint-wrapped ceramics out of duffel bags. She'd painted the Arabic letter *nun* on plates and mugs, surrounded by words beginning with that letter: *We love, we serve, we pray.* "This is the letter they painted on our houses," she said, referring to the way ISIS marked Christian homes in Iraq.

I remember a family so full of questions that they told us, laughing, to spend the night. It was so cold in their rooftop apartment, I never took off my coat. The wife served us silty sweet coffee in tiny cups, then a round of tea in tall glasses. I prayed at the end of the visit, haltingly, blessing them.

One night a woman broke into tears as she listened to a psalm. "Don't cry," my visiting partner, a young taxi driver, said. He felt embarrassed that his reading had made her cry. "It's okay," I told her, putting my hand on her shoulder. "I understand."

In church, the man in front reminds us of yesterday's news: security forces discovered a terrorist cell in Irbid, a city an hour north of Amman. Seven suspects were killed, prevented from using the bomb materials they'd stockpiled. I bow my head, surrounded by these Iraqis who have already answered their doors to ISIS militants, who've been told to convert, pay a special tax, or flee.

I feel rattled. Sometimes it's all too much, too close. I'm a cracked jar of a woman, not really sure how to stand up again, how to keep going. I feel fragile, like someone should put me on a shelf to gather dust for the rest of my life. But here, packed shoulder-to-shoulder with fellow wanderers on this earth, I know that's not right. These are old souls around me. Who can tell what they have seen? And yet they walk on.

When the disciples of Christ told him, "Teach us to pray," he answered with words a child could memorize, simple lines our mothers taught us on our beds. Without instruments, we sing these words in Arabic, some with hands lifted. We remember another world—the lasting one beyond us—then ask for bread, forgiveness. "Deliver us from evil," we pray. I never really knew how to pray this and mean it until I prayed with these people.

In our separate ways, these refugees and I have looked evil in the face and lived. Though hard-pressed on every side, something tells me we can rise together. We do not know what will come, we cannot divine it, but we can press on—all of us deer seeking desert streams, streams to sustain us until we cross the Jordan, until we reach that country where we will weep no more.

CHAPTER 4

A Portrait of Baghdad as Beautiful

Most Americans and Europeans who have gone to Iraq didn't like it at first. Might as well be frank about it. They thought it a harsh, hot, parched, dusty, and inhospitable land. But nearly all of these same people changed their minds after a few days or weeks, and largely on account of the Iraqi people they began to meet. So will you.

—from *A Short Guide to Iraq*,
U.S. War & Navy Departments, 1943

Nejat lived across the hallway from us. We didn't call her Nejat, though—we called her Um Maryam, mother of Maryam, after the niece she'd raised who now lived in Paris and directed a choir. "Goom Maryam," David dubbed her, his two-and-a-half-year-old mouth unable to pronounce the clipped, then stressed letters of *um*.

Whenever we stepped into her kitchen, Goom Maryam threw open her wrinkled arms to him, slack triceps waggling. "*Habibi*, my love!" She engulfed him, grabbing his face in one hand and smacking three kisses on his mouth, each followed by a sound that I, in a whisper, likened to the grunts of a camel. A half-smile rose in David's startled blue-green eyes. He leaned against me and watched her, dressed in a pink and white cotton housedress. David tolerated her kisses because she gave him foil-wrapped chocolates and caramels, cooed and crooned over him. And though we had been neighbors for only nine months, already he chugged his toy trains to Baghdad.

Not that we'd ever been to Baghdad, or that we ever would, the way things looked in 2015, when we moved to Amman and began studying Arabic. In less than a year, ISIS had gobbled up most of Iraq and Syria, establishing Sharia law with brutal force. Sometimes I felt like the world was caving in on us. We felt repercussions in Jordan—Iraqi Christian refugees, who had been threatened with death if they refused to convert to Islam, had settled in our neighborhood in the middle of Jordan's capital. As we practiced our new language, we heard about Baghdad from acquaintances in a variety of settings.

"Baghdad is a very, very, very beautiful place," Um Maryam told me one day in broken *ingleezi* over glasses of sugared Iraqi tea. She sounded like I did in Arabic, multiplying basic adjectives in hopes of communicating meaning. Austin, David, and I had just eaten *tashreeb* at her plastic-covered kitchen table under the ceiling that cried paint chips. We'd closed the front door behind us—a postcard icon of Christ wedged in its speakeasy window—and found her tearing loaves of flatbread into bowls.

She ladled chickpeas, chicken legs, and onions over the bread, and a tomatoey broth flavored with bay leaves and dried limes. She showed us how to press the whole limes against the sides of our bowls to release their sour flavor.

Then, over tea after our meal, she told me about Baghdad again, the place she'd come from in 2007 when sectarian violence had grown hot throughout the country. With her limited English and Iraqi dialect so different from my kindergarten-level Levantine, I basically understood two things: Iraq was hot, and war was real. But I listened, stubbornly responding to her English in Arabic, a habit I developed early on, straining to understand a little more each time. "Baghdad is beautiful," she said. Her description lacked depth or nuance, but it intrigued me, providing a counterpoint to media depictions of violence, offering an alternate view of a place I'd never been.

* * *

I knocked on Um Maryam's door three weeks after beginning full-time Arabic study. She hollered from inside, which I assumed meant, "Come in!" I found her sitting in the living room in front of a gas heater, wearing a turtleneck sweater and a blanket draped over her legs. A dubbed Turkish soap opera played on TV, adding a bit of flickering light to the dim room. In the corner stood a hutch full of crystal. On the walls hung three frames containing Chinese art in pastels.

Inelegantly, I reminded her who I was—that foreigner who'd accidentally knocked on her door before we moved in. Mine was the small blond boy she'd given a banana—did she remember? Yes, she remembered. She spoke in staggering, staccato English dredged up from long ago, when she'd been a secretary and typist in Baghdad.

Emboldened by a homework assignment, I knelt beside her chair and pulled out photographs of my family. "This is my husband. We are married six years," I said in Arabic. "This is my mother. This is my father." I struggled over the words for *firefighter*, *midwife*, and *veterinarian*, all professions in my family. I attempted different vowel and consonant combinations, emphasized sounds we don't have in English. Still I did not communicate.

Um Maryam sat back and looked at me, her sagging face and high cheekbones framed by the gray roots of her hair, which needed dyeing. She raised her drawn-on eyebrows. "Learn Arabic very well," she commanded me in English. After a few more minutes, I left, relieved at having survived an awkward social situation, though a bit unhinged by the difficulty of basic words. What was this beastly language I'd set out to learn, ranked by the U.S. Foreign Service Institute as one of the most difficult in the world?

I decided to visit Um Maryam every week, because she lived alone and was obviously available and because I had language practice hours to fulfill. Eventually, she invited me to sit in the kitchen with her rather than perching on the edge of the salon's stiff upholstery. There I watched her make coffee in the long-handled *daleh*. She hobbled around the kitchen in her black sandals, hunchbacked, gripping the countertop and whispering prayers. "O Jesus, O Mary, help me." (She directed her prayers to Jesus toward the ceiling; Mary sat on a corner shelf on top of a doily.) A doctor said he could alleviate her pain if he could operate on her spine, but there was a 50 percent chance she'd not be able to walk afterward.

"But now I *can* walk," she declared as she poured thick coffee into a pair of cups with knobby noses and painted-on expressions. While sitting at the table, she unashamedly displayed her lower legs to me, mottled red, skin taut, feet crooked with unclipped toe nails. She waited for me to make compassionate noises or comment on their subtle changes, like shifting sand dunes.

* * *

Our family took frequent walks in the evening, a chance for Austin and me to test out verb conjugations and trade vocabulary words. David absorbed the streets quietly—starry white jasmine flowers cascading over garden walls, hole-in-the-wall minimarts stuffed with chips and chocolate and juice, ornery cats pillaging trash. One night at the corner a street down from ours, we exchanged pleasantries with a young Iraqi mom wearing a headscarf. Her chubby, curly-haired daughter and David turned out to be close in age. We swapped numbers, giddily imagining the solidarity of raising toddlers together.

Siham and I spent many afternoons in her apartment. The first time she answered the door without her hijab—frizzy brown curls around her forehead—I didn't recognize her. We drank tea while wrangling David and Rahaf away from the gas heater, which she had barricaded behind chicken wire. Though she had a bachelor's degree in English, she still used Arabic with me. I secretly was pleased by her choice, though I had to pretend to understand much of what she said to me.

Before my birthday in October, she texted me. *Can you help me read a letter from the UN?* After chatting on her living room floor, she left to retrieve the letter. Instead, she returned carrying a full-sized chocolate sheet cake with sliced bananas layered in the middle. "I can't come to your birthday party this weekend," she explained, "so I wanted to make you something instead."

Months later, after Siham had emigrated to Tennessee, I learned that her best childhood memories involved bananas and chocolate, as well as chicken and meat—expensive foods her parents rarely managed to buy in Baghdad in the 1990s. *I still remember one day,* she texted in choppy, unpunctuated English. *My brother saw his friend eat a banana, and since we didn't have money for it, my mom sold old clothes to buy two bananas only.* She told me how Iraqis had suffered under UN sanctions after the 1990 invasion of Kuwait until 2003, how only people close to Saddam had money during that period.

Once, while sitting at Siham's kitchen counter as she scrubbed out a tea kettle, I asked if she brought anything from Baghdad when she came to Amman in 2007. She gestured to a tea glass in the cabinet. I didn't yet have the words to ask, "Why did you choose that glass?" or the alacrity to inquire more deeply. "Why did you come to Jordan? What was the event that caused you to flee?"

Later, from America, she would elaborate. *They wrote on all the walls, if anyone lives with someone from a different sect, they will kill them unless they separate.* Her father was a Sunni Muslim and her mother Shia, so the threats forced them to flee Baghdad. By the time I met Siham, her parents were Swedish residents, having immigrated after several years in Amman. Because she was over eighteen at that time, with her own UN documents, Siham had been left behind.

I met Siham's husband, Mustafa, in pictures. He had returned to Baghdad from Jordan shortly after Rahaf's birth. My Arabic wasn't good enough to understand the reason he had left—that honor had forced him back to Iraq, where he could legally work to pay for the roof over his wife's head and for his daughter's formula instead of depending on his in-laws' kindness. I couldn't yet understand how they'd met online and that Rahaf wasn't their first child. (Siham later explained how she miscarried after their landlord evicted them because they'd been forced to wander on foot all day in search of affordable housing.)

Siham and Mustafa talked through the Internet now, and Rahaf smiled and squealed when she saw her *baba*. Even though she didn't know what Baba smelled like, what it was like to hold his hand, she knew he was her daddy.

* * *

Who was I more than half my life ago, when I lived in rural California and Baghdad was just a capital to be memorized, when Iraqis were not my next-door neighbors? I want to reconstruct myself accurately, to honestly resurrect a former self. And so I remember: September 10, 2001, when I was fourteen, my geometry lesson included a picture of the Twin Towers. The next day, when they collapsed, I was unaware of how their fall would shape my future and vocational interests, how instead of repelling me from Muslims, this event would draw me to them like a magnet.

Shortly after 9-11, President George W. Bush gave a speech to Congress, using unfamiliar words like al-Qaeda and terrorism, caricaturing America as "freedom itself under attack." That's what we all believed, our grieving selves who were avoiding airports but braving work and grocery stores with flags clipped to our cars. "As long as the United States of America is determined and strong, this will not be an age of terror," Bush said. "This will be an age of liberty here and across the world."

As I watched Fox News with my parents that fall, the idea of war felt heavy, something from history textbooks. I watched recent high school graduates from our blue-collar community ride waves of patriotic fervor. Several guys—riotous, flirtatious all—enrolled in the Marine Corps and vanished to boot camp in San Diego. A few months later, they returned, tall and straight as bayonets, wearing wooly uniforms with buzz-cut hair. These guys stood in church to grateful applause, then shook hands with older people in the lobby while girls like me shyly observed from the corners.

In March 2003, I sat in my room drawing the latest Fox News banner in the margins of my journal: *Operation Iraqi Freedom.* The Bush administration told us that Saddam Hussein, the dictator of Iraq, was hiding these things called weapons of mass destruction, that he was a threat to our freedom like the terrorists in Afghanistan who we'd been fighting for two years. Iraqis needed a democracy like ours, the government informed us—and after all, who wouldn't want a government like ours?

"This will not be a campaign of half measures," President Bush said in a televised speech at the beginning of the U.S. invasion of Iraq. "We will accept no outcome but victory. . . . We will defend our freedom. We will bring freedom to others. And we will prevail."

Siham was fifteen, a high schooler like me, when American troops entered her country. Before the invasion, she didn't understand why so many people wanted Saddam ousted. No one talked about him. They knew his reach was far, that criticism could bring reprisals. When kids left for school in the morning, their parents cautioned, "Don't say anything about Saddam."

In 2003, Siham saw American soldiers walk into stores in her Baghdad neighborhood with friendly smiles and gifts or candy for kids. *We thought Iraq would become like America*, she confessed. *We lived around one year without water or power, but we were looking to something in the future.* Around a year later, public opinion shifted. Siham began to see insurgents in her city—armed civilians rising up against American occupation. Dead bodies of those who dealt with Americans became a common sight.

Meanwhile, as a high school senior, I sat in a room full of other students, blank paper and pencils on a table before me. We had two hours to answer this question in a bid for a college scholarship: *What is your definition of a hero?* Sweaty-palmed but focused, I outlined my essay with three answers entirely shaped by 9-11 and its aftermath: firefighters (among whom my father was one), American troops ("They are fighting to create freedom for the Iraqi people"), and George W. Bush (who pursued "the liberation of Iraq"). I won $4,000 for that essay, and my parents, so proud, mailed a copy to the White House. Bush replied with a letter typed on thick, creamy paper with a foil-embossed seal. He thanked me for my essay. He praised me as a young patriot.

In Jordan, with Um Maryam's front door two yards from mine, with Siham around the corner and a building full of Iraqi Christian refugees across the street, I felt embarrassed—regretful that I once won money for lauding Bush's decisions. "Bush ruined the Middle East," Um Maryam told me once, plain as day. When I considered this possibility out loud in Arabic class—"Is the mess we see in Iraq today my country's fault?"—my teacher responded quickly. "Well, that is well-known."

But I am also able to reflect on my teenage self gently. How could I—or the Bush administration, for that matter—have anticipated the disastrous results of the U.S. invasion? In 2003, very few Americans had the insight to know that the blueprint of American democracy wouldn't fit over Iraq. No one foresaw that the overthrow of Saddam's rule, though cruel, would lead to worse things. And no one knew that one day America, the nation that vowed to bring freedom to Iraqis, would try to ban them from finding it on her shores.

While giving David a bath one night, I received a string of worried questions from Siham. Some in Congress wanted to block Iraqi and Syrian refugees from entering the United States. Deep in the application process to emigrate to America, she wanted to understand why. *What do these decisions mean?* I read, phone screen fogging under my dripping thumbs. *Why is the government doing this?*

When I was seventeen, I had lots of words—words that won me money. I had the surety, the black-and-white answers that come with physical distance and lack of meaningful engagement. But when questions like these came from my friend while bathing David next door to Iraq, all I had were two words: *I'm sorry, I'm sorry, I'm sorry.*

* * *

Between our first and second semesters of Arabic study, Austin and I met with a private tutor to read the Gospel of John in Arabic. After our first session, I sat down, placed an index card under the first verse, and tried to read. But reading to yourself is abysmal when you don't know what you're saying and whether you're saying it right.

So I went to Um Maryam. "First drink coffee, then study," she commanded when I asked her for help. David sat on my lap as Um Maryam boiled grounds, water, and sugar. While we sat and sipped, she made and received calls on her red, candy bar-sized phone—brief morning greetings to neighbors, the pharmacist, the corner shop owner, friends she could no longer access because of crippling pain. I listened, watching the minutes tick by on the wall clock. Local pop and oldies floated from her boombox on the counter. The gas truck passed our building with its tinny, music box tune, followed by staticky shouts from the vegetable vendor's megaphone.

By this time, I could speak a little more, ask a few more questions. "Why did you not marry?" I inquired, aware that an unmarried woman her age was rare in Arab culture. Both her parents had been sick with cancer, she informed me. Because she was their only daughter, her father had refused the marriage proposals of ten men—she held up both hands—so she could stay and care for them.

"And now I am alone," she concluded, ruefully.

But if David and I came, I reasoned, she wouldn't be alone. We could liven up her well-worn routine with the action and noise she craved. She could listen to us like we were the news— the sometimes unintelligible but busy and incarnate news.

Without air conditioning, the kitchen was hot, even in the morning. Sometimes the faint, citrusy scent of Dettol, Um Maryam's favorite antiseptic, filled my nostrils. After struggling three or four times through a passage in John, Um Maryam would slip off her reading glasses and wipe her forehead with a rag, sip from a sweating bottle of ice water. Then we'd lean back in, her finger tracing the lines for me, urging me on and on. "*Afiyeh*," she said after I crawled through particularly knotty words. "Bravo."

Bonded by our twice-weekly reading sessions, Um Maryam began to call me every day. "How are you?" she asked. "What did you do today? What did you cook? Where did you go?" I tried to think positively. I should feel loved by her regular check-ins, right? Mostly, though, I felt smothered. I talked to no one daily, not even my own mother. When her questions proceeded into a rapid-fire string, I felt trampled, manipulated. "Where are you? Where were you this morning? Why didn't you come?"

Sometimes I didn't answer my phone because I didn't know how to respond. Occasionally I had the foresight and courage for simple statements. "Um Maryam, I love you, but I can't come every day." Usually, though, I just felt guilty. She heard us whenever we left our apartment. I started to hush David in the stairwell when we returned. Um Maryam was a radar speed gun, and she gave me a ticket every time I entered and exited my home.

The Arabs around me couldn't seem to understand how beaten down I felt by language learning and cultural adjustment. Trips to the grocery store didn't deplete them. They couldn't fathom how nervous I felt standing at the butcher's counter, rehearsing how to ask for my whole chicken to be cut in fourths. They didn't know how much attention I mustered in the dairy section, scrutinizing labels so I would choose milk and not the salted yogurt drink, or how unstable I felt in the produce section, standing in front of *kusa* with a glowing blank in my mind where the word *zucchini* once sat. Arabs didn't experience the bombardment of signage on storefronts and road signs, the labor of reading text messages and preschool announcements.

And I didn't understand them sometimes. Why didn't anyone return my visits? Sets of tea glasses and coffee cups sat unused in our kitchen cabinet. Why did our new acquaintances never seem to follow through with their plans? One neighbor had proposed a visit to the Dead Sea. Another had invited me to cook with her. Why did they use the forceful imperative so often in their speech? Why did Siham take hours to reply to her messages? *Are you upset with me?* I texted, scrambling for some response, anxious for proof that my friendship mattered to someone.

After five hours of Arabic class, a five-minute interaction with Um Maryam felt impossible, to say the least. When I tried to express that to her, I sounded infantile. There were probably thesaurus columns full of the words I kept repeating. "I feel very, very tired because of the life in a new place."

I prepared soup one night in my kitchen that had exactly one drawer and less than a square yard of counter space. The sound of Um Maryam's ringing phone drifted through our shared wall. I had to express myself better, I decided, had to flush out my thoughts and emotions even though I felt incompetent. I constructed a possible conversation in Arabic, then practiced out loud.

"Um Maryam, I love you." I knew how to say that. I chopped an onion, minced garlic so fresh it made me cry.

"I want to see you. I know your life is hard because you are alone." I peeled carrots, chopped them into coins. "But I can't visit you every day."

It hurts to say no, it hurts, but I have to. I flinched inwardly. *I have to if I'm going to live.*

"I have responsibility in my home—" *Am I saying that right?* "—and I have to study, and I want to see my other friends." I shook cumin into the pot, salt and pepper, a little cayenne.

"I don't know what your expecta—" *I don't know that word in Arabic.* "I don't know what is normal here, but in my culture . . ."

When I poured water on the vegetables, they protested with loud sizzling, then went silent. My nervous mind continued to blister. *What will she say? How will she react?*

* * *

I experienced my first flashback in May 2016. While walking alone on the roads of my parents' California neighborhood, a dog crashed against a fence, growling and barking. Suddenly I was being assaulted again, swallowed by the shock of that February morning in Amman when a teenager in a black hoodie put his hand between my legs, spoke words I can't remember, and ran away. I knew I was safe in America, but my mind could not disengage from the terror. I pulled my scarf over my head, sat on the side of the road, and wept. A half-hour later, I told my parents, "I feel like I just came back from Iraq."

Eventually, after weeks of intensifying insomnia and anxiety, I was diagnosed with post-traumatic stress disorder. I first heard of this mental illness as a teenager, something applied to soldiers returning from Iraq and Afghanistan. Maybe that's why I said what I did to my parents after the flashback, even though I'd never been immersed in combat. Austin, David, and I spent an unexpected year in America, sequestered in a mostly empty building in the Midwest while we tried to sort out what had happened to me and how I could recover.

While stateside, I dreamed in Arabic two or three times a week. These weren't the nightmares characteristic of PTSD, but they did highlight my obsessive love for Arabic and my concern for Um Maryam, who appeared in almost all of them. When I described my relationship with Um Maryam to a therapist, she suggested codependency. Perhaps in Um Maryam's loneliness she had controlled and taken advantage of me. Perhaps in my yearning for acceptance and approval, I had capitulated too often to her expressed needs.

Initially, the therapist's idea felt off-base. Later I cried angry tears, realizing that some of my exhaustion resulted from poor boundaries with my neighbor. I had made myself more vulnerable to trauma by my inability to say no appropriately in a culture that often depends on indirect communication.

As I recovered, I found myself prowling around libraries to learn about Iraq. I remembered the many Christian Iraqi families I'd visited as I practiced Arabic, people who endured years of sectarian violence and finally fled the death threats of ISIS. What had they thought of their country? Did they, like Um Maryam, have memories of its beauty? And what had Um Maryam meant by the word *beautiful*? Had nostalgia discolored her view of reality? No doubt Baghdad contained physically beautiful places—the Tigris River lined by palm trees or the famous book market on al-Mutanabbi Street with the century-old Shabandar Café. But had she referred to this or to another kind of beauty?

And so I read, haphazardly but widely: a book by a journalist who traveled in Iraq before the Gulf War, the diary of an Iraqi teenager at the time of the U.S. invasion, poetry about Baghdad from ancient times to the present. In verse, the ancients praised Baghdad for its beauty, but all recent memories were of war. Sinan Antoon wrote of searching for future peace and instead finding "a mother weaving a shroud / For a dead man / Still in her womb."

I checked out a collection of interviews about Iraqis' lives after the U.S. invasion but had to shelf it. The stories were so heart-wrenching and gruesome that I couldn't continue until I was strong enough. The book's spine caught my eye each time I passed our bookshelf on the way to the bathroom, where I frequently filled the tub with hot water and lavender oil to relax my body.

Eventually, I picked up the book again and read Maysoon Mahdi's account of a deadly attack on her bus route. She quoted a verse from the Qur'an that she said Muslims sometimes use as a prayer for safety: "[We] have placed a barrier before them and a barrier behind them and covered them up so they fail to see."

Had Siham ever whispered this verse under her breath when, as a teenager, she walked past dead bodies on the way to school? I thought of Um Maryam's words again. *Baghdad is beautiful.* She had seen death and lived through wars before Siham and I were even born. What did her words mean?

In another book, written by a journalist who spent time among Iraqi Christians, I saw a picture taken in a school for Iraqi refugees in Amman. A framed drawing held the trauma of a child, neatly labelled by a teacher: war planes that looked like finned hot dogs; a black, red, and white flag ("Iraq Flag burnt from isis," the caption said); a black cloud with red underneath ("explosion"), a couple of *nuns*, the letter ISIS spray-painted on Christians' homes. A stick figure had an open mouth and a red pool near his neck ("the man died"), and another had frowning eyebrows and a smiley face ("isis happy").

Miraculously, this page had a second half: a sun in the upper corner, a perfect ROY G BIV rainbow arching over a fruit tree simultaneously bearing apples, oranges, and lemons. A small building ("my home") sat opposite a big one ("my church") and a row of stick figures carrying presents ("the people in the church come to help us"). The last caption expressed the child-artist's conclusion: "my life in Jordan full of save happy."

After studying this picture, I meditated on how resilient humans are. Our bodies are so fragile; a tiny piece of metal to the neck can take us from this world. But our spirits—they can go through hell, not just once, but day after day after day, and still they live. After shock and suffering, we can recover. I was living that reality—albeit on a much smaller level than the Iraqis I knew. I was living one day at a time, trying to care for all the parts of myself, in hopes that the health of one part would facilitate and promote the healing of others.

While taking medications, going to counseling, and doing yoga in the Midwest, I didn't know I would eventually volunteer for the organization that founded the school for Iraqi children in Amman where that child drew his or her picture. I didn't know I'd partner with Lillian to visit refugees, Lillian who had been a member of the Ba'ath Party, spoken to Saddam Hussein on multiple occasions, and worked as the personal seamstress of multiple high-ups in the Iraqi government. I'd meet Munir, an Iraqi man who could have been a model with his aquiline nose, low-lidded eyes, and day-old stubble. Munir, who worked all night in a factory, hoping he'd get paid at the end of the month, and then came out to visit his countrymen with us. Sometimes in the car he and Lillian would melt from Arabic into Syriac, an ancient language spoken by some Iraqi Christians. "I can't understand you!" I'd protest.

We visited so many hardy people. I think of Suha's mother sitting in the living room's half-light. Paint sloughed off the walls in places where it'd been slathered to hide mold. A plaited cross of palm hung beside where the elderly woman sat, whispering Syriac expressions of love to Christ, her beloved.

An extended family from Basra received us many times, the men wearing long dishdashas, the women completely shrouded. Once Lillian lifted Ahlam's and Leena's face veils to determine who was who. I learned to distinguish them based on their eyes and voices, their hands and feet, which were usually stained with red-brown henna. We drank Turkish coffee from porcelain tea cups, or tea with an inch of sugar, and Ahlam served us bread made in her kitchen. One of Leena's daughters would hardly speak because she'd seen the unspeakable. Once I brought a bunch of yarn and needles and taught them to knit, even the boys. One day Um Khalid chuckled, "I never would have dreamed that I'd be in Jordan sitting with an American."

I don't know what Um Maryam meant when she expressed her longing for a beautiful Baghdad of the past, but I began to see its meaning for me. Baghdad was a microcosm of the whole nation, and I clearly perceived beauty in its people. I had been received in dozens of homes whose Iraqi tenants consistently welcomed me with smiles and kisses. Never accusations, never snide remarks—just coffee and cookies, which spoke, "Your nation destroyed ours, but you are our guest. You are a person like us, and you are welcome." I saw wounded spirits able to extend hospitality and kindness, traumatized hearts that still loved.

If that's not beautiful, I don't know what is.

* * *

A year after her immigration to Chattanooga, Tennessee, Siham called me. Donald Trump had been president not even a month and had already halved the number of U.S. refugee arrivals and issued executive orders barring Iraqis and Syrians from entering the country. I answered the phone in our Midwest kitchen, and for the first time in our friendship, Siham and I spoke in English. I felt like I was talking too fast, my words tumbling out in an excited torrent. Siham was working for a phone company and had recently been promoted to office manager. Rahaf was in a daycare and speaking English more than Arabic.

"I liked Chattanooga from the first minute," she told me, "because it was my last station—no more waiting, no more thinking about Rahaf's future. It was the place to start my life in the right way." Many people had helped them, and she found most Americans to be friendly. If people didn't like her, she was empathetic. They only knew what they'd heard about Iraqis, not who she really was.

"The only thing I need now is Mustafa," she said. We didn't discuss how that might be impossible under Trump's administration. Mustafa's face was the one I saw in that season of travel bans and broiling anti-refugee sentiment. I wished people could see who he really was: a husband and a father, a human.

In the midst of that gray Midwest winter, Siham reinforced what I was already observing. In spite of the dead bodies she'd seen, the wars and poverty, she—like many Iraqis—was still open-hearted, eager to adjust, full of hope for her future. Though she'd lost her family, country, and language, she found a way to flourish in her new home. She was like a seedling sprouting after a forest fire or like the phoenix of myth. Her life had gone up in a roar of flames, but rather than letting scars debilitate her, instead of turning inward, growing callous, or shutting down, she was being born again.

* * *

As I write this, it's been more than eight years since I met Um Maryam and two and a half years since she died. Hers was the first dead body I saw not in a coffin. I touched her still face, kissed her head, experienced that strange lack of response, its finality. Two men carried her quilt-wrapped body out of the apartment on a stretcher. I watched from my doorway with baby Adam on my hip.

Her decline was long. Before we traveled to America in 2016, she strained a muscle when setting a full bucket of water outside her door for Ibrahim, the Egyptian who cleaned our building's staircase. She stayed in bed for four days, was forced to urinate in a pan and call someone to take it away for her. The doctor who lived upstairs came to examine her. Our downstairs neighbor brought her plates of food.

"Why doesn't your family come?" we all asked, no one clear about the exact nature of her family's problems. In a culture where unmarried women never live alone, Um Maryam was an anomaly. "Shame on them for treating you like this," the neighbors said, invoking cultural principles and indirectly expressing their weariness, their inability to care for her in light of their own responsibilities. She really needed twenty-four-hour care. I'm not sure any of us realized how thick were the lies of normalcy she hid behind, how she didn't trust her brothers enough to expose her true condition to them.

Before we traveled to the States, before she started scooting around in a wheelchair, David and I dashed over frequently. "I need my phone charger," she called to say. Or, "Come, lock the door for the night and keep the key with you."

We entered her dim bedroom with yellowed chiffon curtains, enormous wooden wardrobes filled with clothes she no longer wore, and sat next to her on her bed. She lay on her side, the hard lump of a Bible underneath her pillow. As we chatted about our day and giggled over David's latest antics, I felt like we were at a sleepover or a campout. Um Maryam was enjoying the attention. And while I felt fulfilled in being so useful, eventually I dreaded how long she'd be bedridden. I anticipated how my quick responses to her needs would only deepen her dependence on me.

We didn't know then how this injury foreshadowed her final fall. Though she could walk again by the time we returned from America in mid-2017, a year later Austin and David heard her cries while returning from school and found her on the floor with a broken hip. Though I learned through counsel and reflection how to say no, how to pursue healthier ways of relationship, I would be forced to love anyway—to help her in the shower when she feared slipping unattended, to lift her to the commode and wipe her after she went to the bathroom. She was so dignified in these humiliating moments. Cold sweat broke out on her face, but she was not overly apologetic or embarrassed but rather graceful.

When I consider her now, I realize what an injured spirit Um Maryam had—one blunted by her parents' selfish treatment, her brothers' neglect, the isolation of being housebound. I marvel at how she chose to love anyway. All those plates of saffron-colored rice studded with beef, chicken with dill and green fava beans, the supply of caramels she kept just for David, the consistent calls. Maybe loving gave her reason to live. Maybe these were her acts of resistance against a crippled body, the way she prevented the paralysis of her spirit.

I could look back at my former self and be critical about how I didn't know my boundaries, how I too often let compassion and guilt control me. But maybe my responses were loving through wounding too. Maybe sometimes we face situations so desperate and difficult that injury is inevitable. Then we must choose to be kind even though it hurts. What are the boundaries of kindness anyway? When do we try to limit love? Can't affection and dysfunction exist together in relationships and love cover a multitude of sins?

All I have of Um Maryam now is a stolen picture. She never wanted to be photographed, she was so vain. But when I saw her, couch-bound and frail, holding my little Adam for whom we'd waited together, my heart contracted with joy. Her hands were like bird claws around him, a fleecy blue bundle, and her hair had grown completely gray. The rusty tube of a catheter snaked out from under the floral quilt covering her legs.

Inconspicuously, I titled my phone upward in my lap and snapped an image.

CHAPTER 5

Slowly, Slowly

The face is my goal—*al-wijh*—and though as a barista I pulled thousands of crema-crowned espresso shots, this, my friends, is different. On first attempt, my coffee stares up at me without a hint of creamy face. Flat, like a soda without carbonation.

When I ask our Jordanian neighbors about it with my newly acquired past-tense verbs—"I made coffee, it had no face"—the room bursts with suggestions. "The water was too cold." "You didn't give it enough time." When I tell my Iraqi neighbor I used coffee from the supermarket, preground and prepackaged, she clicks her tongue at me. *No.*

Well. What's a girl to do? I follow my friend Alia into a store with open bins of spices, nuts, and candy. She blesses the employee and orders seven ounces of medium roast coffee with cardamom. He chooses beans from the middle of a spectrum and throws a few cardamom pods into the grinder after them.

The next morning, we sit on her couch, sipping it sweet, looking at old sonogram photos of her daughter.

I change my method. At home, drink American coffee in big mugs with milk. Outside, drink Turkish-style coffee made by people who know what they're doing. The strategy applies beyond coffee-making too. Inside, speak English and act how I want. Outside, watch and listen and relearn what I've known for years.

Watch Medihah make coffee on the two-burner stove in her bathroom, where a little vine crawls through the tear in the window screen. Listen to the boiling water pop above the blue gas flame, the spoon scrape round and round. See how she pours the coffee gently, though it sizzles and spits in protest on the hot sides of the long-handled metal pot. She murmurs a word to soothe this coffee tantrum—says it with a smile, like a mama watching her toddler throw a fit.

Shway, shway, the Arabs say, slowly, slowly. It's a motto for life here, a way to live. Stop living by lists and scheduling; throw your goals out the window. Move slowly, slowly, or the coffee will sense your hurry and hide its face. *Shway, shway,* or the cardamom won't have time to sink, and you'll catch its piney grains in your teeth. Slowly, slowly, or you'll wear yourself out with vocabulary before you've even begun, or you'll skip admissions that you don't understand, or you'll be running so fast you'll miss the joy. Your neighbor will turn your empty cup onto its saucer and tap the sludge down to read your fortune, and it will not look good for you.

Watch Um Mohammad's Bangladeshi housekeeper. Her back to you, she soaps up the coffee cups while chatting in

Arabic, and you remember Naomi Shihab Nye's lines: "Until you speak Arabic / you will not understand pain." The problem is, you feel pain and still you do not speak. Jealousy cuts deep. The triple devils of comparison, competition, and condemnation rip you raw.

Shway, shway, they tell you, but you do not want to go slowly. You gulp your coffee, clawing for the lowered inhibition and speedy synapses caffeine promises, driving your desire for properly paired nouns and adjectives and unbotched verb conjugations. You want the voice of a bulbul. Like a nightingale, you want to open your mouth in full-throated song.

It will come, they say. And it *will* come, believe me, but only after you fall out of the nest—because someone knows you need humbling, a radical pruning back, if you're to have a chance at flourishing. You'll fall far and hard and spend a time flapping your naked wings in the dust, blind. You'll lie limp with your heart jumping out of your chest, watching your vision of your fluent, trilling self die.

And then someone will pick you up, set you back in your place. You'll wobble forward gratefully and figure out how to live. You'll learn to sip your coffee, to say, "I don't understand." You'll learn to catch your mistakes tenderly, in two hands, to release them without self-flagellation. You'll allow words and expressions, dialects and idiolects to flow over you like water. You'll walk along, slowly, slowly, until one day, in your neighbor's kitchen, you'll pour a cup of coffee with a golden face—proof that everything will be all right.

PART 2

Meditation

CHAPTER 6

Attention

The desert demands attention from my eyes trained to praise the lush wet and green, the accessible and abundant, which do not require attention, so here where a woman stands on the side of the road in abaya long and dark backdropped by olive trees thirsty for harvest rain, I give attention by setting my screen aside and seeing the whole palette of yellow and brown, distinguishing between a bushy star thistle needing more attention than a burgeoning globe thistle, and I submit to the desert's demand for attention because I read this week that attention is prayer and I need so much to pray like the outrageously blossoming spires of sea squill standing attention under the sky that has not opened in months, and like the shepherd in jeans and checkered shemagh giving close attention to his sheep scanning hillsides for stubble, and because

attention is prayer, for the first time in my life I feel
the need to study these crusty backbones of sediment
laid bare and these fracture caves that maybe housed
hermits devoting full attention to heaven and these
blocks of limestone once fortress where a wheatear
hopping black and white draws my attention and I
approach slowly, focusing on its most basic colors
rich and bold under the sky which calls attention
upward to these plains of Moab, where God wooed
the children of Israel wandering and sitting in their
tents at attention waiting for manna to coat the
desert like coriander and snow sparkling like this
stone, and now I walk this wilderness demanding
attention, quiet, eyes, and I know why monks retreat
to the desert to delete the distractions capturing
their attention, to baptize themselves in the bleach
of unblinking sun and let every lark and squill and
wheatear and thistle arrest their attention and split
their souls open to cleansing and accepting every gift
gratefully in their dust-cracked hands.

CHAPTER 7

Into the Rugged Unknown

*The life [the Bedouin] lead is the life their forefathers
led before them. They accept hardships and privations;
they know no other way. . . . No man can live this life
and emerge unchanged. He will carry, however faint,
the imprint of the desert, the brand which marks the
nomad; and he will have within him the yearning
to return.*

—Wilfred Thesiger, *Arabian Sands*, 1959

Mohammad pinched sprigs from a plant nestled
between the rocks, then tore up half of a dried bush.
On the craggy, southern-facing slope near Wadi
Feynan, I knew by his movements that we'd be stopping for tea
soon. We'd been climbing with his flock of goats for an hour
and a half. The shepherd wore tattered, synthetic sandals that—

paired with experience—climbed the rocks more steadily than my sneakers. I focused on the ground for several more yards until we reached a bald outcrop of rock overlooking the vast canyons and mountains of the Dana Biosphere Reserve.

Mohammad and I had met that morning in a dry riverbed near Wadi Feynan's off-the-grid ecolodge where Austin and I had spent the night. Jordan's Royal Society for the Conservation of Nature modeled the lodge off of historic caravanserai, desert rest-houses that lined regional trade routes in centuries past. We woke early to the twittering of sparrows nesting in the hotel's eaves, then ate breakfast prepared by the lodge's employees, all members of the local community. Around nine, we ventured out to find the Bedouin shepherd I'd signed up to spend an entire day with.

Though the lodge's website advertised the option of shepherdesses for solo female travelers, the front desk staff had said no, there weren't any shepherdesses available. I'd lived in Jordan for six years and was used to adapting culturally. That included the Islamic custom of separating unrelated males and females at weddings and funerals, during home visits, even in many primary and secondary schools. I'd never dreamed of crossing this societal boundary, of doing something so nonconformist. I felt a twinge uneasy as I set off with Mohammad and his nameless, putty-colored donkey for eight-plus hours into the unknown.

As Mohammad and I walked up the riverbed, I tried to muster all the cultural respect I could. I told him I had two sons and that he could call me Um David—mother of David. Mohammad replied that he was also married and had two daughters and a six-year-old son named Jawad.

"How old are you?" he asked.

"Thirty-five," I replied. "How old are you?"

"Thirty."

I glanced at him with a smile. "Then I am your older sister."

* * *

On the stony outcrop, Abu Jawad—father of Jawad—
arranged the dry bush he'd uprooted in a rock ring, then pulled
a lighter from one of his donkey's saddlebags. As he laid out the
tea things—a half-gallon jug of water, a charred kettle, sugar,
and loose-leaf tea—he made a confession.

"Usually they let me know the night before."

When he set just one tea glass between us, I realized why
Abu Jawad felt compelled to apologize. The ecolodge staff hadn't
informed him that I'd be joining him for the day, not before
they'd pulled him off the path on his way to work. He washed
the small glass with water, dried it with a corner of the red-and-
white checkered shemagh covering his hair, then poured me the
first cup.

I picked up the handleless glass by its rim with thumb and
middle finger and placed it on the rock in front of me. How many
hundreds of cups of tea and coffee had I drunk with women and
families in Jordan, sitting cross-legged like this, wearing this
same skirt even. This was certainly different though. Before me
stretched the majestic view, beside me sat the man in a black knit
sweater and ratty navy sweats mended with white thread.

As I sipped tea steeped with the feathery herb he'd picked
on the path, Abu Jawad and I ate a simple breakfast: *shraak*—
thinner-than-tortilla flatbread, made by his wife—and whole

tomatoes. In the absence of a knife, I watched him dig in his thumbs to split the fruits in half. I copied him, gelatinous seeds and juice coating my fingers. When I had drunk three cups of tea (he insisted on the third), I told him it was his turn. He poured himself a glass, then leaned back on his elbow, legs stretched out.

We waited for the herd of goats—seventy to eighty animals— to catch up with us. Already, one of my basic assumptions about the shepherding profession had been broken. While I assumed a shepherd stayed close to his animals, determining their path and keeping them out of trouble, Abu Jawad just got them going in the right direction and then walked far ahead of them, stopping every twenty or thirty minutes to wait for them to meander his way. *Is that because these are goats, not sheep?* I wondered.

My head felt packed with questions, including a basic one that seemed to have an elusive answer. "What makes a Bedouin a Bedouin?" A middle-aged traveler at the ecolodge had asked that the night before. Is someone who lives in a tent, pursuing a nomadic lifestyle, necessarily Bedouin? Or is it more a matter of lineage, tribal association? And what might be the connection between Bedouin and modern Jordanian identity, I wondered? Just a tiny minority of Jordanians still practice a nomadic lifestyle, but I noticed that traditional Bedouin culture and values were promoted and celebrated as most authentically Jordanian.

In a hefty volume by Syrian writer Jabril Jabbur, I read that before modern borders, Middle Eastern nomads commonly raided villages to demand *khawa*, a tribute paid in exchange for protection. Roaming tribes also competed for grazing land and watering holes for their flocks of sheep, goats, and camels. One of Jabbur's premises grabbed my attention. "The Arab does not know himself, or understand his unique qualities and the range of his capacity for development, if he does not know that the way he lives has its roots in the desert." Maybe I *was* onto something by questioning the connection between the traditional Bedouin life and modern Arab culture.

From where we sat, Abu Jawad and I could no longer see the Feynan Valley, an area southeast of the Dead Sea. The night before, Austin and I had hiked around the Roman-era archaeological site slung over with globular black slag from the copper mining industry that had thrived there in ancient times. We saw ruins of three churches dedicated to Roman-era Christian martyrs who died there while working in the mines. As the sun set, we overlooked a silver ribbon river spidering through the wadi, irrigating fields of watermelon and tomato bushes. Around forty-five Bedouin families still lived in tents in this area, Abu Jawad's family among them.

The quiet around me was immense. I could hear flies, my body's own static, and far, far away, the rustling of the goats as they approached.

* * *

While Abu Jawad drank his tea, I took out my notebook and started jotting down observations. For years I'd nursed a curiosity about shepherds, wondered how I could talk with one in a culturally appropriate way. During Jordan's blitzkrieg spring, I saw shepherds everywhere, especially on the grassy hillsides outside of Amman. Even in empty lots in the city, sheep and goats grazed right beside roaring traffic.

The COVID-19 pandemic had spoiled a much-anticipated chance to spend an afternoon with shepherds in the north. So imagine my delight when I discovered that Feynan's ecolodge offered "A Day with a Shepherd." I fairly chortled with joy. My sister, who was visiting from the U.S. when I found the opportunity, laughed at me. "I can't believe you want to do that!" she exclaimed. "Especially after our childhood with goats."

My sister was right—we'd spent a whole lot of time with goats. As pre-teens growing up in the mountains of California, we owned two black-and-white pygmies. We loved incorporating them into our imaginative play on our parents' five-acre parcel—herding them around with sticks and playing "shepherd girls." But we also were disgusted by their stench and how they never stopped eating. They gorged themselves on grass and weeds, becoming visibly bloated and then letting off all kinds of gas. Also, they were stubborn. Also, they were not agreeable. They pretended to be macho, sharpening their stubby horns on tree trunks and fence posts, then head-butting one another and sometimes us.

When Abu Jawad's goats arrived below us, he stood up. He grunted and whooped, whistled and hissed to guide the multi-colored herd. A couple of times he banged a section of plastic pipe on a rock to get their attention. If a goat was not walking in the direction he wished, he aimed a rock to land beside it. When they weren't nose-down, snuffling out tender plants or succulent bits of thorny ones, the goats flowed over the rocky landscape. Abu Jawad told me this was one primary difference between sheep and goats. By virtue of their anatomy and size, goats are much nimbler. They can traverse territory that is difficult for bulky sheep.

We quickly packed our breakfast things and continued our walk. My long skirt snagged on rocks and bushes, and I was glad I'd worn leggings beneath it. I also was glad I liked vigorous walking. It seemed that shepherding, at least in this rugged country, mostly involved walking. Though I had a hard time imagining this kind of physical activity day after day, Abu Jawad seemed content with his work. "It's not tiring," he said. "You relax."

I puzzled out the form of this Arabic verb—not "it relaxes you" but "you become relaxed by it"—and walked behind him and the donkey, led by a frayed plastic rope.

* * *

Granite, limestone, sandstone, basalt. These four types of rock form the mountains and valleys texturing the eastern side of al-Araba, the north-south valley between the Dead and Red Seas. I have an avowed dislike of geology—give me living, breathing flora and fauna, not dead rocks—but here in Jordan, taking a preliminary interest in stone seems unavoidable. As I walked behind Abu Jawad, I tried to at least pay attention to the minerals and sediments beneath my feet. (My nine-year-old could do better.)

Dislike of geology aside, these stark cliffs have entranced me for years. When I first saw the wilderness areas east of Jerusalem as a nineteen-year-old studying abroad, I felt unexplainably attracted to them. They are so different from the California hills descending from my mountain town to the city below—those hills that are close to my heart, unrivaled in my mind: gentle, soft, and yellow, dotted with sleepy-looking oaks, their ridges unfolding like heavy blankets settling in the wind.

Those were the mountains of my teenage memory, of drives to Costco and ballet class. But those wilderness mountains in Israel were in a category of their own, their rough majesty like a knife cleaving my childhood and adult consciousness. I saw the Bedouin working in the sharply cut wadis and wondered about their life in tents. Curiosity burned in me; I couldn't take my eyes off their encampments.

When I returned to work for the same study-abroad program in my early twenties, I always enjoyed the day we drove the students from Jerusalem to Jericho, plunging to 846 feet below sea level. I'd stare out the bus window at February's green frost on the hillsides, at September's bare nothingness.

When we moved to Jordan, I found its wilderness even more grand than that of Israel. The cliffs of Moab and Edom were cocoa, smoke, and thunderclouds. Light and shadow imprinted them with so much detail, it was almost too much for my eyes to take in. Clumps of palm nestled among these rocks—not gangly, naked-to-the-head Southern California palms, but misty, feathery green ones with sprays of *balah*—unripe, orange dates—peeking out.

As we trekked up a ravine, Abu Jawad pointed out a leafless shrub with turgid stems. *Anabasis articulata,* I later read in my field guide, which Bedouins pound until foamy and use as soap. We scrambled down to a low, sandy place with lots of shrubs, where dragonflies cruised the air. The shepherd motioned to a human-placed rock border that enclosed a space at the bottom of a slope. A place to plant seed, he explained as we passed by.

Every time we stopped to wait for the goats, I had more questions for Abu Jawad. I knew the Bedouin speak a different sort of Arabic than I had learned in the city, but I didn't expect it to be so dissimilar. I'd grown accustomed, perhaps, to interacting with guides who work closely with tourists, who are constantly exposed to the Ammani accent. Abu Jawad, though, used different vocabulary than I, even for sheep and goats. I understood about 50 percent of his words, which made my questions multiply faster than I could ask them.

* * *

The goats weren't far behind us. They pranced and galloped over the rocks with their long ears flapping, flickering tails curled upward. When we stopped in a green wadi, they emerged from behind rocks, popping out to stare at me with amber and honey eyes while chewing round and round. They were suspicious of me, it seemed. And I don't blame them. Who wouldn't be suspicious of someone who chuckled at their disgruntled and complaining bleats?

"Let's make a pot of milk," Abu Jawad suggested. He selected a black goat from the herd and pulled her over, clamping her back foot under his arm. Grasping a leathery, gray teat, he milked her right into the kettle. After adding a generous scoop of sugar to the foamy milk, he heated it in the campfire he'd built.

He told me how the Bedouin milk their goats and make butter, *samn*—the Bedouin version of ghee—and *jameed*—dehydrated yogurt—from it. These products can be sold for profit, in addition to the meat of goats taken to markets. The Bedouin themselves never have to buy meat; all their needs are supplied from their herds. They cut the goats' hair once a year, in May or June, and traditionally use the black hair to weave their tents. But not many people do that anymore, Abu Jawad noted, as they can purchase commercially manufactured structures.

While we drank sweet milk, the goats rested in the shade. I guessed it was around one o'clock and figured this was the halfway point of our journey. (I snuck occasional time checks on my phone, which was stashed on the donkey and had no reception. Abu Jawad, however, did not carry a phone or wear a watch.) When we packed up our things, we turned south again, vaguely in the direction of Wadi Feynan. While we walked at the bottom of a dry riverbed, the goats traipsed along the mountainside far above us.

* * *

When we stopped at a sandstone concave to rest, Abu Jawad whooped once, his shout echoing back a half-second later. The goats' bleated response shivered off the rocks. Abu Jawad lay down with a rock as a pillow while I sat with my back against the wall. A tree stood before us with a pair of sunbirds perched inside. I heard the sound of a cuckoo bird, migratory in this area, and the whir of rising chukar.

Close to four o'clock, we took another rest. The goats were far from us, out of sight, but they somehow knew the general direction of home. Was it the slant of the sun, habit? Abu Jawad wrapped his face in his shemagh and lay down for a nap. I had nothing else to do, so I decided to rest too, though it felt immensely strange to nap alongside a man. I positioned myself a yard or two away from him and stretched out on the dirt.

I listened to the birds and wondered what my life would be like if I spent my working days without phone or Internet, alone in the cliffs and canyons. As Westerners, we're fascinated by this pastoral lifestyle, by the idea of independently living off the land. We wonder what it would be like to live without the restrictions of schedules, the metal and glass structures that cage and master us. *But is this vanishing life truly idyllic?* I wondered. *Should we idolize it? Do the Bedouin want change, or are outside institutions and constructs forcibly preserving this group's way of life?*

When the goats caught up—all swaying ears and udders and wattles—Abu Jawad took a deep breath. A cloud of flies rose from his scarf. When he opened his eyes, he surveyed the goats engulfing him, then looked back at me with a grin.

"When you get home, do you count them?" I asked.

Abu Jawad surveyed the crowd around us. *"Inshallah,* God willing, they are all here."

* * *

In the widening gulch of Wadi Feynan, a camp emerged. Abu Jawad and I approached a cluster of three tents where two barefoot old women sat sunning themselves. I was surprised by how happy I was to see other women, how, as usual, women's voices were more comprehensible to my ears than men's. I noticed how good touch felt to this mama who was used to being a toddler's jungle gym. One woman wore a jacket over her head, preventing me from getting a good look at her face, but the second, wearing a floral headscarf, had faded tattoo marks on her chin and jaw, traditional Bedouin markings.

I figured we were just passing through, until Abu Jawad ducked into one of the tents. I eagerly followed. The shelter was a reception area of sorts, just several yards square with a pit of hot ashes in the center. The walls were pieces of woven plastic stitched together. A hole in the upper corner admitted a smoky shaft of light.

Abu Jawad and an elderly man reclined opposite me, the lady with the jacket sat in the dirt, and the woman with the faded tattoos, who had a tiny, bent frame, insisted on making tea. She retrieved water from a group of jugs outside, then set the tea pot in the ashes. Soon it was engulfed by flames. She handed me half a piece of *arboud*, the thick, chewy bread Bedouin make in the desert by baking a mixture of flour, salt, and water buried in hot ashes.

I overheard Abu Jawad and the older man chatting.

"How was she?" he asked.

"Energetic," Abu Jawad replied, to my delight.

A slender young woman approached from outside. I greeted her in Arabic, which piqued her interest and drew her in. She settled down across from me, wearing a baseball cap tied down with a maroon headscarf. Her skin was lighter than the older women's, taut across her facial bones, yet her front teeth were browned from tea. She was a shepherdess—Abu Jawad's sister-in-law, I later learned—and she asked where we'd been today. The little old ladies exclaimed about how far he'd taken me.

"I was behind you all day," the shepherdess told us with a smile.

* * *

I perceived Abu Jawad was ready to continue home. I tucked my unfinished arboud into my skirt pocket, and we walked down the road, now wide and passable for vehicles. I had more questions for the shepherd: What do you think about all day? Do you ever feel lonely? I've heard shepherds don't have a good reputation in Arab society—is that true? I hesitated, partly because I knew I wouldn't understand his answers, partly because I knew those kinds of questions would cross an intimate line. Perhaps it was better to keep things practical, introductory for now. I sensed this was the only the beginning of my Bedouin explorations.

Across the riverbed a woman wearing a black dress with flashing rhinestones called to us, her shape dramatic against the world turned yellow by the setting sun. She and Abu Jawad shouted back and forth to each other. I wasn't sure how they understood one another, their words tumbling up and down the sides of the canyon.

"She thinks you're my sister, Aisha," Abu Jawad said, looking at me. "Call to her."

I did a tap-dance inside, like I do whenever I'm mistaken for a local—like when drivers pull up alongside me to ask for directions, when my accent conceals my American roots, when my premeditated clothing and accessory choices hide my foreignness. I've acclimated enough to trick people into thinking I'm one of them, though at my core I still feel foreign.

"Hello!" I shouted to the woman in Arabic. "How are you?"

Against the vast landscape, my words sounded thin, insufficient—but I was understood.

CHAPTER 8

Warp & Weft

Men are the wool of the tribe, but women are the ones who weave the pattern.

—Arabic proverb

Um Ayman's hands are skilled. I watch them as we sit in an open-air tent beside her one-story house in al-Diseh, a village in southern Jordan. Her skin is the color of cinnamon, her nails hennaed a rusty orange. She wears an intricate ring on her left hand and three rose-gold bangles on her right wrist. The bracelets clink musically as she fastens yarns to a Bedouin-style ground loom, presently just two pieces of doweling secured by bent rebar pounded into the earth.

We've selected seven colors for the warp threads of our woven piece. Five are synthetic yarns purchased from a shop in Aqaba, Jordan's southernmost city. The other two are natural yarns Um Ayman spun herself, off-white from sheep wool and black from goat hair. She asks me in which order I'd like to arrange the threads; I make a few suggestions but eventually defer to her. My suggestions feel full of guessing compared to those of this fifty-year-old Bedouin woman who grew up in a goat-hair tent.

I will spend the next three mornings with Um Ayman, participating in a customized weaving workshop. My general interest in Jordan's Bedouin had grown laser-sharp. I wanted to meet women, who seemed, at least from an outsider's perspective, nearly invisible. I'd seen evidence of them in a tiny heritage museum in downtown Amman, where I admired their handwork: woven rugs used to separate one exhibit from the next. In the Jordan Museum, alongside a diagram mapping Jordan's major tribes, I'd studied a row of black dresses embroidered with tribal designs. They were like ghosts—or rather, the empty trappings of souls long gone.

After eight years in Jordan, the only traditional Bedouin women I was conscious of interacting with were several in Wadi Feynan and Abu Sultan's wife, with whom I exchanged halting greetings during our family's first visit to Wadi Rum. In the sandy yard of their home, she served us sweet black tea steeped with sage. She appeared only briefly, a mirage.

The vast majority of Jordan's Bedouin now live in brick-and-mortar homes, but from books, I was aware of the tremendous role women had played in nomadic life. Jabril Jabbur wrote that nearly every task required of a nomadic family fell into their capable hands: cooking, collecting firewood, raising children, packing up camels, pitching tents, milking goats. I read of pregnant women giving birth on the move, pausing to deliver their babies, then wrapping them and continuing to walk. I saw a picture of jameed—hand-shaped balls of tart yogurt used to make *mansaf*—dehydrating on the roof of a tent. I saw women in voluminous dresses, some with hair plaited into long braids, weaving tent panels on rocky ground.

They were like the exemplary woman of Solomon's proverbs. In the conservative Christian community in which I was raised, some had lauded this Proverbs 31 woman. Girls had aspired to the identity of "keepers at home." A few families even rejected the idea of higher education for girls, believing they instead should stay home until marriage, serving their families and practicing the homemaking skills they'd use as wives and mothers. The Bedouin women I saw in photographs—literal builders and bakers and weavers—seemed embodied examples of the virtuous woman those girls in the 1990s had sought to become.

The woman King Solomon describes in couplets has glimmers of Bedouin all over her, just like the woman in Songs of Songs— a sturdy, dark girl climbing craggy mountains after her flock:

> She selects wool and flax,
> and works with eager hands.
>
> She sets about her work vigorously;
> her arms are strong for her tasks.
>
> In her hand she holds the distaff
> and grasps the spindle with her fingers.
>
> She is clothed with strength and dignity;
> she can laugh at the days to come.

* * *

British anthropologist Shelagh Weir ultimately led me to pursue weaving as a portal into the lives of Jordanian Bedouin women. "Weaving is the only developed craft among the bedouin [*sic*]," she wrote, adding that "the craft is entirely in the hands of the women."

As Um Ayman knots a synthetic brown yarn to the straight doweling at one end of the ground loom, I'm grateful for the opportunity to learn a craft pushed toward extinction by factories and mass production. My instructor walks to the far end of the loom, unrolling the yarn as she goes, then loops it around a second doweling before returning to the first. She continues like this, back and forth in her black stockinged feet, making figure-eight loops until a taut stripe of brown traverses the loom's length of two or three yards. These are our warp threads, the lengthwise yarns that create the foundation of a woven piece.

"Now you try." She hands me a ball of sheep wool yarn. It's bulkier than the synthetic stuff, coarse with wiry fibers standing out. I walk down the loom's length, copying her movements. "Like this?" I ask in Arabic.

After about an hour, Um Ayman sits at the halfway point of our extended warp threads and uses a ball of yarn to separate and lift half of the threads above the others. Two cinderblocks, one on either side of the warps, elevate these threads, which are secured to a horizontal piece of wood by looped placeholder yarns. She shows me the shuttle wound with gray-brown weft thread, hand-spun from camel and sheep fibers, and the beam used to beat down the weft—the yarn a weaver laces between the warps. Over time, the oils of her hands have smoothed this piece of wood like the back of a well-handled kitchen chair.

"This is the only piece of the loom a Bedouin woman keeps," she tells me. "Everything else can be improvised in a new place."

* * *

In an Amman strip mall near one of the city's few pork stores and one of its only gluten-free bakeries, Khalil Naouri runs Shiraz Stores. The middle-aged Jordanian and I sat at his desk in the shop's back corner, surrounded by Orthodox icons and replicas of keys to Palestinian homes abandoned in 1948. Nearby, among antique coffee-making implements and hutches embedded with mother-of-pearl, sat three piles of weavings almost as tall as I. They looked like they were dyed yesterday.

"The most important thing in Jordanian heritage is weaving," Naouri told me, echoing what I'd read in Weir. "It's the house, the bag, the mattress, the way the Bedu stayed warm. All of their lives were centered around weaving."

Though he's from an old Jordanian family, Naouri didn't start to notice local weavings until the early 2000s. Since then, he's traveled to all corners of the Kingdom to research weaving. Historically, Jordanians practiced the craft in two styles: Bedouin women used ground looms, and men, usually in the northwestern villages, used upright looms. After gathering specimens from twenty-three tribes, Naouri published a photographic catalogue of his collection, a visual tribute to the hardiness and creativity of the Jordanian people.

"The picture that the West has about the Bedu is that they are a simple group, backward . . . but they don't see an important aspect," Naouri said. "These people, they are survivors. All the civilizations came from them."

The life of Bedouin women in particular wasn't easy. Naouri demonstrated how women would squat to cook and weave. They always had pieces of weaving in process, continually working on tent panels to replace those worn from exposure and weather. But tent production wasn't their only work. The rugs, pillowcases, and storage bags inside the tent, as well as the saddlebags and reins for camels and horses, were woven as well. All of these were seen by guests, from within the tribe or without—and the quality of their work reflected the status and strength of their tribe. Women didn't just weave for shelter and survival; weaving was an art, a way to express their identity.

Naouri held out his hands to me while describing Bedouin women's palms. Goat hair is wiry and cuts the skin easily. In the absence of moisturizers and lotions, weavers' hands developed thick callouses that enabled them to work with wool. "You'd feel that their hands were torn and dry," he said. "The palms of their hands were like wood. This was their strength."

* * *

Um Ayman sits at the end of the loom, pulling the weft thread between layers of raised and lowered warp threads. As she works, her black chiffon scarf occasionally slips from her head. Her hair is still mostly brown, threaded with gray like mist on mountains. She has fine wrinkles around her eyes, a full lower lip. The mole above her mouth is a beauty mark some women would pay for.

As she weaves, she tells me she got married at seventeen and has nine children. She tells me about her mother, who still lives in *bayt as-sha'ar*—a house of hair, as the Bedouin call their tents—twenty-five or thirty miles east of al-Diseh. The elderly woman has no electricity, cooks over a fire, hauls in water, and tends to the family's animals. Her personal belongings hang in a bag on the wall of the tent. Um Ayman speaks of her matter-of-factly, with tacit acceptance of how her lifestyle has modernized while her mother's remained.

Um Ayman learned to weave by watching and assisting her mother, who has made three complete tents in her lifetime—a massive labor considering tents can be sixteen yards long and four wide. She remembers living in these as a girl—black-and-white striped panels stitched together with thick thread, pitched over poles and fastened down with guy ropes. On windy days, the tent flapped and occasionally collapsed on them. When it rained, water sluiced in. Constructing the tent—from production of the woven panels to spreading and erecting it—was entirely women's work.

"The Bedu life is work and rest," Um Ayman tells me, using the Arabic equivalent of the English word Bedouin. "Physical work and mental rest." She grasps a hook and plucks the weft thread, cinching it closer to the growing piece of fabric. Then, after several passes of the weft, Um Ayman puts down her tools. "Do you want to try?" she asks me.

I kneel at the end of the loom and immediately feel incapable, lost. Where do I put my hands? Um Ayman helps me. First we press the upper set of warp threads down and lift the lower ones. When I was given a loom as a child, I accomplished this with a light plastic heddle, lifting all the warps effortlessly with one hand. Separating these threads feels like a wrestling match, like combing through a forest.

"The problem is the synthetic threads," Um Ayman observes after several minutes. "See how stretchy and thin they are? They're sticking to the natural fibers."

After a short while, my thighs are burning and my arms fatigued. Bashfully, I switch places with my teacher, stationing myself nearby with a glass of tea and my notebook. *Weaving is not going to be my thing,* I think, feeling slightly deflated. It seems I don't have the sheer strength and flexibility required for the job.

Maybe I can't weave, but I can chat. One of Um Ayman's sons sits nearby on the plastic mat covering the dirt. His dark hair sticks straight up like it's been hair-sprayed, though I'm guessing he just got out of bed. He wears wire-rimmed glasses, camo pants, and a NASA sweatshirt with an American flag patch.

"Oprah is here today," he says.

"Really?" we all exclaim.

"And Princess Iman with her new husband."

"They came to Wadi Rum for their honeymoon?" someone comments incredulously.

Um Ayman's oldest son strides into the tent, lean and muscular. He wears an amusing-to-me combination of nomadic and modern dress—a dishdasha with sneakers below and a baseball cap on top. After bending to kiss his mother's head, he sits near me to talk. When his preschool-aged son appears, I listen in on their conversation.

"What's this?" Ayman asks the boy, holding up a smooth, straight stick. It's crowned with a bulb of wood that's implanted with a metal hook.

"A tree?" the boy guesses.

"No, a *maghzal,*" Ayman replies. Maghzal, Arabic for spindle. I record the word in my notebook.

"He can make a whale sound," Ayman says proudly.

Hearing this, the boy meows like a cat, throwing us all into giggles.

Abu Ayman enters next, a short, rotund man wearing a sport coat over his charcoal dishdasha. He's jolly and tender toward the grandkids drifting in and out of the tent. Once he realizes I speak Arabic, Abu Ayman sits cross-legged and answers my questions with exaggerated hand gestures.

"Before the '70s, al-Diseh was not here," Abu Ayman tells me, launching into the history of his village. Though the Jordanian government had encouraged the Bedouin nationwide to settle since the 1930s, King Hussein especially promoted sedentarization in the '50s, '60s, and '70s. He built wells on the fringe of the Wadi Rum protected area and opened schools and health centers to serve the nomadic population.

At first, the nomads pitched their tents around the wells and began to dabble in agriculture. Then they built houses. Today, around 10,000 Bedouin live in the seven villages ringing Wadi Rum's northern edge. Al-Diseh, mainly populated by the al-Zwaydeh tribe, boasts a two-lane thoroughfare lined with grocery stores, pharmacies, bakeries, and a community center. Several laundry establishments take advantage of Wadi Rum's tourism industry. On the drive to

Um Ayman's home, I saw lines loaded with freshly washed sheets and towels.

"Tourism has given to us and taken from us," Abu Ayman says. "It gave us openness and education, but it took the simple life."

Later that day, I savor this simplicity while playing with David and Adam in our camp, a ten-minute drive from al-Diseh. The boys romp barefoot on clean sand, shelter in sandstone caves, smash orange and purple rocks, and slide headfirst down dunes. Without cars, streets, or trash, the possibilities for exploration and play are endless—boundless opportunities for sleuthing and sliding, digging and bouldering. Mothering feels easier here, with all this room to roam. They don't ask for screen time, don't bicker, don't get grumpy from being caged indoors.

Honestly, parenting here also feels easier because I spend half the day away from my kids. In Um Ayman's tent, I'm invigorated by my role as observer, reporter, and writer. I relish the hours away from the boys, hours of creative exploration uninterrupted by whining or disputes.

Now, tromping west to catch the sunset, I recalibrate to engage with my sons. I aim to play rather than dwell in the cerebral, where I'm continually developing questions, shaping phrases, and gathering information into sentences. At home, emerging from writing work is difficult. Familiar surroundings and repetitive activities bore me and keep me seeking refuge in my mind. Words dribble out everywhere—in my planner, on the back of receipts, in notes on my phone. Adam shouts across the apartment when I tarry too long in another room. He knows when I'm distracted.

Here in Wadi Rum, we're all captivated by the desert, which makes the transition from writer to mama easier. Distant pickups flash on crisscross paths across the vast magnificence of multicolored sand, flanked by rock formations resembling melted candle wax or frosted cupcakes. Shadows of moisture from this week's rain crease the shaded crevices and north-facing slopes. Pale lavender flowers come up in damp gullies, trembling in the breeze. Waxy leaves unroll like curled ribbons. I pause, enchanted, at each new variety, these flowers in the desert so improbable.

* * *

I recently visited three generations of Jordanian women in Ma'an, a low-slung city on the Desert Highway. The U.S. embassy regularly cautions Americans from entering Ma'an, prone as it is to hosting riots and anti-government demonstrations. Yet this city also has a long history as a rest stop for pilgrims making their way to and from Mecca, and normal people live there— human beings who eat and work and sleep and need medical care. I accompanied a social worker friend on home visits to her clients, severely disabled children and adults.

The home we visited was unique—a cluster of rooms circling a courtyard, where the winter sun made everything bright as a bleached *thobe*. Inside, a second-year university student named Zara sat beside me, somewhere between girl and woman. She wore braces on her teeth—one of the brackets mounted on the tiniest nub of an upper tooth—and she wanted to know what sort of cosmetics I use to keep my skin clear. But she also described how she had shouldered the care of her grandmother during a recent hospital stay and explained to my friend about her brother's seizures and medications. Then she brought her tablet from another room to show me some poems she was studying as an Arabic literature major.

"Do you want to be a teacher when you finish?" I asked.

"A teacher, yes, but more than a teacher," she replied.

"You're ambitious," I told her, leaning over to playfully press her knee, "like me. I want to be a mother, but more than a mother."

"I want to leave a mark on the world," Zara stated, using the Arabic word for fingerprint. Retucking her black scarf near her cheek, she continued. "I want to leave something so I'm remembered when I'm gone."

As our gaze drifted to her half-siblings, smushing and rolling playdough on baking trays, I was reminded of the war with ambition I fight every day. On days filled with cleaning, laundry, meal planning, and shopping, I sometimes feel a half-person, discontent with being only a housewife and mother.

I watch Zara's mother, whose husband's second wife lives across the muddy lot from here, and her grandmother, lying in bed under several garish, faux mink blankets, a C-PAP machine wedged beside her. These are hardy women. Doubtless they're of Bedouin descent, probably born and raised in the wilderness. Zara's grandmother most likely can't read, but her hands raised children, raised livestock, raised roofs. I don't know if she longed for more than these traditional roles, but at least she did what her culture required.

Maybe my problem is this: I've lived in such a hodgepodge of communities and value systems that I don't know what's required of me. I was nurtured by a mother who sacrificed years of her career to educate me and my siblings at home. As a teen, she supplemented my physics and logic courses with books about marriage and womanhood. Although she offered me biblically conversative views, Mom also helped me identify and develop my gifting as a writer and prepare me for college so I could have a career if I wanted one.

Even so, after I married Austin, I needed time to adjust to the idea of my mother-in-law, who had successfully worked full-time *and* raised three children. Was such a thing possible? With my husband a full-time graduate student for the first six years of our marriage, I didn't have the leisure to parse out ideas about women's roles. To support him meant working—and I was glad to. I made coffee, freelanced articles, and scrutinized oversized page proofs at the kitchen table while baby David napped. In the Chicago suburbs, our neighbors were mainly Burmese refugees. In some families, the wife worked the day shift and the husband the night.

Then we moved to Jordan, where most mothers I know stay at home. The West's ideas of contemporary roles have certainly pricked the Arab world, but development toward these ideals has been far from absolute. Women comprise the majority of university students in Jordan, but they also shoulder the bulk of responsibilities in their homes, with husbands and sons as the primary breadwinners. They work hard in their private domains, no doubt about it, tutoring their kids under the education system's punishing standards, mopping their tile floors with a regularity that puts me to shame, and cooking meticulously crafted meals—hand-cored zucchini stuffed with rice and meat, enormous pots of hand-rolled grape leaves.

In Jordan I noticed the severe judgment one might incur if found incompetent as a homemaker. When one neighbor, a divorced mom who worked full-time, moved out, another woman commented scornfully about her housekeeping. "It's like a man was living there!" she said. I shied away inside, uneasy about what she might think when she entered my home. I noticed how some Arabs still judge a woman by her ability to produce children, sons in particular, and how having two sons didn't make me immune from literal imperatives to get pregnant.

Let me put this straight. I do find satisfaction in maintaining a home for my family. Routine tasks like sweeping and vacuuming and pinning wet clothes to the laundry rack soothe me with their repetitive nature. And the surge of love I feel when Adam and David dive into bed on either side of me, when I cradle their shaggy blond heads as they squirm and tussle like kittens—it's unparalleled.

But I also feel relief when I close the door behind them on school mornings and click on the tea kettle before sitting down to work. Is something wrong with me because I feel that way, because I want more than motherhood? Because I find equal— or often more—fulfillment in writing and volunteer work? Do the interviews, articles, and essays that occupy me while the boys are out make me a less excellent woman than my Arab friends who devote themselves to raising children and creating immaculate homes?

Alan Keohane, who extensively photographed Bedouin communities across the Middle East, suggests that Bedouin women adapt more easily than men to their morphing world because their duties are indispensable. Since "homemaking and the rearing of children are unchanged," the Bedouin woman has a stable core, he argues. She doesn't struggle with a changing identity to the extent of her husband, who can no longer occupy himself with activities like raiding and shepherding, so central to Bedouin identity.

But what of the women who don't want to remain static, who desire to branch out from their historic roles? What about Zara? Will society treat her harshly if she breaks with centuries of tradition, if her inner nomad leads her wandering to higher education, full-time employment, or an untethered, unmarried life?

Cradling my glass of tea beside Zara, I observed the generations of women packed in a tiny room and wondered, *What can a woman's hands do?*

* * *

Um Ayman's hands are skilled. On our second morning together, after sipping thimblefuls of Saudi coffee—creamy, almost yellow—she produces a clump of wool, washed and carded but still raw, a cloud in the hand. She holds the spindle before me, the one Ayman's little boy called a tree.

She tugs a bit of the wool out, teases it into a column, then twists it down tight and hooks the end to the spindle. With the loose wool in one hand, she places the spindle on her thigh and begins to roll it up and down her leg. Yarn forms, spinning out of the cloud like a rope of rain. I've seen black-and-white pictures of Bedouin women occupied like this, with fat sacks of wool slung on their shoulders. Abu Ayman told me how women used to spin yarn while tending goats or walking to a new campsite. "They always took advantage of time," he said.

"And now we're always on our phones," I comment to Um Ayman with a smirk.

Brenda, a Dutch woman who's lived in the desert for fifteen years and who introduced me to Um Ayman, pipes in. "We've lost something in our day," she says, her voice soft. "When we want to do something with our hands to let our minds rest, we pick up our phones. But they don't empty our minds."

Though we come from three continents, Um Ayman, Brenda, and I lament how our devices fill our marginal minutes, not with calmness but with messages that demand responses, with status updates and headlines that fritter and fray our attention. Handwork like spinning and weaving has therapeutic power, we observe, the ability to restore minds in the midst of productive labor.

Weaving reminds me of the times I helped my Jordanian Christian neighbor make *ma'amoul* for Easter. We prepared ourselves mugs of Nescafé, turned on an Egyptian movie from the 1950s or the Mass broadcast from a church in Lebanon, and settled on her couches to form the holiday cookies. We spoke little, our common, rhythmic activity sufficient conversation. Pinch balls from a bowl of coarse semolina dough. Fill hollowed dough nests with a paste of pulverized dates and spices, or of walnuts with cinnamon and sugar. Crimp designs reminiscent of lace with a pair of tongs, designs that represent Christ's thorn-pierced brow. Punch a single hole in the middle of each cookie, symbolizing his nail-pierced hands.

Making ma'amoul soothed the mind like weaving—unlike the tasks that often occupy me as a working woman. My mornings can be frenzied, with hours of screen time and toggling between messaging apps. Sometimes I feel consumed by work, the burn to be productive while David and Adam are at school. Pausing between tasks for even a minute feels Herculean. Sometimes I forget to breathe.

I regret what the technology-driven world has stolen from me and so many women: the contentment and satisfaction that can spring from sustaining others' lives with our hands. Might my encounters with Bedouin women like Um Ayman help me reclaim the value of my vital roles as mother and wife? Can I go home with a renewed sense of purpose, knowing that what I do there is important?

Brenda, Um Ayman, and I work while al-Diseh sleeps. We separate warp threads and pass the weft between them before plucking it down. Bit by bit, a band of woven fabric grows beneath our hands. I'm not yet sure what to call it—a table runner, a wall hanging, a placemat? Outside, a fuchsia bougainvillea near the house crackles softly in the mid-March breeze. Roosters crow and birds twitter in the tree that spreads over the tent. We pause our weaving before noontime prayers. I head for the desert camp, wishing Um Ayman a blessed Friday.

* * *

After writing a profile on Jordan's first lavender farm for a local paper, I returned to Burayqa, a northern town of about 1,000 inhabitants, to meet the owner's mother. According to her daughter-in-law, Um Shalal was "Bedu and proud." She greeted me with a squeegee in hand, her pineapple-spangled housedress bundled into the waist of her leggings.

"Let me finish this," she said, gesturing to soapy puddles sloshed on the tiled corridor.

When she joined me on the ornate couches in her formal living room, Um Shalal talked about the Bani Sakher, one of Jordan's most well-known tribes. In the 16th century, they came from the Arabian Peninsula searching for water and food for their animals, migrating as far north as Syria. She feels proud to be part of such a prominent, respected tribe, reflecting a community-based honor universal in the Middle East.

Um Shalal described her childhood living between tent and village, recalled the fear she experienced as a girl because of a violent feud between her father and his cousins. She married young, her father-in-law paying her bride price with his end-of-service bonus from the army. Her husband was a truck driver who delivered vegetables to countries as far away as Kuwait, Turkey, Oman, Iran, and Israel. Like many other Jordanian Bedouin, several of her sons and daughters have worked in public service positions, including the army and civil defense.

Though she grew up in a traditional lifestyle—even baking bread for her fifteen children before Burayqa had a bakery—Um Shalal now has a smartphone and uses social media. "I've lived between the past generation and the current one," she said.

"Kind of like a bridge?" I suggested.

"*Aywa*," she agreed—an emphatic, Jordanian *yes*.

Being with Um Shalal makes me think of my paternal grandmother, also mother of fifteen children. (I mention my enormous family to Arabs regularly to bash their impression that all American families are small. "One wife, no twins," I emphasize.) By the time I was old enough to remember, my nana was hollowed by Alzheimer's disease. I saw her in a nursing home bed once, when we accompanied my Pendelton-clad grandpa on his daily visit.

I like to imagine how strong Nana must have been—just 4 feet, 11 inches tall but able to conceive, gestate, and nourish fifteen children in the span of twenty-one years. Surely she wasn't a saint, but I have no one to prove me otherwise. I'd like to ask her about making lunches for more than a dozen children, about hand-sewing dresses with rick-rack and ruffles for my aunts. Surely she didn't have time to read at night, much less build a career. Motherhood was her career.

If I parented exclusively, I think I'd be pushed to the edge of insanity. My mom-only brain would lie fallow, unused. But at the same time, as a full-time writer I'd be ragged, choked—a different kind of useless. So is it possible that my vocations complement and balance each other? Is it actually a gift to be both writer and mother? If so, how can I faithfully integrate these callings with more gratefulness and less self-condemnation?

I recognize that I need to confidently accept the culture Austin and I are creating in our home. I need to put aside insecure or self-conscious thoughts brought on by comparisons with other women and relax into the reality that in our family, Mama does not need to keep a perfect house. I want to embrace the fact that I am invigorated for housework by stewarding my God-given gifts of compassion and creativity, to affirm the truth that my work outside the home gives me more joy for the work within these walls.

I need to accept this integrated version of myself: A mother spending two hours of solitude with her laptop and a drafted essay. A writer eating toasted cheese sandwiches on the back porch with her son. A mother jotting thoughts on paper while answering her boy's questions. A writer hanging laundry before returning to her notepad, now decorated with her son's scribbles, which spark in her a little firework of happiness—because she is a mother.

* **

There are Bedouin women who live like me too—employed both inside and outside of their homes. Several months after weaving with Um Ayman, I sat in Udhruh, a village several kilometers outside of rose-red Petra. Um Abdulrahman told me how, for several hours each morning, she picks tomatoes in nearby fields. After she fulfills her quota, she returns home to cook and care for her eight children, two of whom are disabled. Then, after finishing her housework, she sits at her ground loom to weave eight to sixteen inches before calling it a day.

Um Abdulrahman wore black—headscarf, abaya, and all. Her thin face seemed a combination of young and old—fine wrinkles mixed with quick, animated expressions. I sat in her guest room with three other women, all of whom supplement their incomes by working for a company striving to revive Bedouin-style weaving.

The other women contributed to our conversation, but Um Abdulrahman was easily the most dynamic. As she told me about her girlhood in the desert, she tossed her arms to illustrate hanging wet laundry on tent poles, baking paper-thin wheat bread on a domed pan called a *saaj*, chopping firewood with an axe, and milking goats. Her frame was slight but her gestures larger-than-life.

"I love the desert—everything about it," she exclaimed. She recalled brewing cups of tea and then climbing a rise to watch the sunset, of following herds into the basalt-strewn desert, shining like the bottom of a drained ocean. She recounted how every night her father connected their television to the car battery so they could watch the eight o'clock news and a show before sleeping at nine so they could wake with the animals at sunrise.

"But," she transitioned, "the day I moved into a house—"

"And you got a refrigerator, a washing machine—" the oldest woman interjected.

"—it was amazing."

The house we sat in was adequate but lacking by middle-class Jordanian standards. Um Abdulrahman told me it was remodeled from a unit built by King Hussein during his efforts to settle the Bedouin. Paint flakes from the walls, and the ceiling leaks during storms. Inside the front doorway, down a chipped concrete step, her loom stretched out, constructed of repurposed metal pipes. The only furniture in the guest room was a cabinet storing bedding and cushions around the walls. A window with textured, cracked panes opened to a square of sunset sky.

I think of the contrast between this home and the tent of Um Saleh, a middle-aged woman who welcomed me to her family's encampment during Ramadan, a month after my workshop with Um Ayman. She grinned with curiosity as I parked, her hands balled in the pockets of her sporty abaya. Behind her, a verdant strip of mallow grew beneath a satellite dish planted in the packed ground.

Though she was fasting, Um Saleh cheerfully led me into their main tent, spacious with eight-foot ceilings. Barefoot, we passed through the first room, the domain of Abu Saleh and his male guests. A small iron stove anchored the space, its flue jutting out of the tent's roof. I touched the sloped ceiling, composed of three layers: feed bags sewn together by hand, a layer of cardboard, and outermost, a layer of factory-manufactured, black-and-white tent material.

"It took a month to sew it all together," one of Um Saleh's daughters said, noting my interest in their shelter.

I sat with the women and babies and bottles in the second room, on the other side of a Spiderman sheet. I smiled wryly; I knew that one hundred years ago this divider—the *saha*—would have been the most intricately woven piece of the tent, a statement of the occupant's status. At the far end of the tent, behind another sheet, the family stored blankets, cushions, and clothing. A mama cat trotted out from behind the sheet, followed by five wobbly kittens with scraggly tails and startled, newly opened eyes.

Half-sheepishly, I asked if Um Saleh would show me her kitchen, a place normally off-limits for guests. She laughed as we walked to a smaller tent featuring a free-standing cabinet on which sat two burners and a pressure cooker. Non-perishable foods were stashed behind curtains. Um Saleh pointed to a slouching pile of animal feed bags in the corner.

"They were just delivered," she explained apologetically.

Outside, the setting sun chiseled detail on the barren land around me, every rock and dry bush thrown into relief. Desolate grazing lands stretched endlessly in all directions. A quarter-mile to the east, eighteen-wheelers barreled down the Desert Highway. In addition to the 350 sheep and goats grazing with

Abu Saleh's hired shepherd, a few hundred more idled in open-air pens near the family's encampment. I breathed deeply the smell of animal dung and rain-rinsed air.

The women in Udhruh understood this lifestyle. Besides Um Abdulrahman, two others had grown up in tents—and they reassured me that their Bedouin essence hadn't changed with their change in housing. Generosity, high self-esteem, hospitality—they claimed all these characteristics over the din of shrieking children, clattering cups, a metal door slamming, teenage girls answering phone calls. *Shahaama*, one of them added, a word an Egyptian friend later defined as chivalry, nobility, courtesy, courage, and kindness all rolled into one. I recognized endurance among them as well—something unbroken and strong in their bold and boisterous spirits. *She is clothed with strength and dignity,* Proverbs said. *She can laugh at the days to come.*

"It doesn't make a difference that we've settled in houses," one woman noted.

"We have customs and traditions," another cut in.

The first continued. "We are still Bedu—our customs and traditions haven't changed."

"All of this village is Bedu," Um Abdulrahman elaborated. "If a guest comes to someone, they'll be received like they were in a tent."

"So the only difference is the wall?" I knocked on the cinderblock behind my head.

We all laughed. "That's the difference!" they agreed.

* * *

Months after these encounters, an image rises in my mind like a key to a map. That strange house in Ma'an, inhabited by Zara and her mother and grandmother—maybe it was a metaphor for ways of being. A cluster of rooms surrounding a whitewashed courtyard, each with its own doorway to the light. A picture of the various ways women can successfully function in this world.

On our final morning together, Um Ayman's thirty-five-year-old daughter Rimas visits. Like the hands of every Bedouin woman I meet, hers are full. She has five children and teaches second grade in a nearby village. Her eyes make me think of date syrup. With her headscarf removed, she sits cross-legged on the ground with the tent pole at her back and a cooing baby in her lap. I hear the blunt clicking of the weft hook in Um Ayman's hand. Behind us, Rimas's kids argue animatedly over their card game.

"Cheater!"

"All the hearts go together."

"No, not like that!"

As we chat, Rimas occasionally points out where some of our warp threads are misplaced. She can't weave entire pieces like Um Ayman, but she knows enough to recognize mistakes. I sense mutual support between Rimas and her mom, just as I noticed respect and acceptance in Um Ayman's attitude toward her still-nomadic mother. Um Ayman's hands wove Rimas's world, and as Rimas builds her home—through very different but respectable work—her mother is there to lift her up. This family is a web of diligent women who need each other.

In the yard, I hear a swing squeaking on rusty hinges as a cold front swoops in from the north. Um Ayman cuts the warp threads to release our woven project, now about a yard long. She, Rimas, and I handle it, laughing over the stark difference between my work and Um Ayman's. They bundle the weaving into a plastic bag, along with some bright pink and purple yarns. "You could make tassels for the ends," Rimas suggests. As we hug and kiss one another, they wish me a safe drive to Amman, and I leave, a bag of handwork in my grip.

CHAPTER 9

Table in the Wilderness

Growing up in Southern California, my sisters and I played in a backyard olive tree. The tree—a single root ball branching into multiple, outspreading trunks—acted as the cradle of our imaginative games. If the mood was right, it transformed into a boat in which we sailed to the New World like explorers and pilgrims. Other days it became a shelter for us as Indigenous Americans or pioneers.

Once, after Dad trimmed the tree, we used its branches as building material, weaving walls into the jungle gym he had salvaged from a local preschool and installed beside our swing set. Though the supple branches splintered green when cracked, woven together they created a structure so sturdy we could rest on it like a bunk. I remember the powdery silt left on my hands after handling the olive leaves and branches—a dustiness that seemed alive.

With these core memories of our olive tree—larger-than-life and open-armed—I was not surprised when, twenty-five years later, I heard the word *grace* applied to olives.

David perched on the lamppost in front of our Amman apartment with a container of olives, waiting for street cats. To my chagrin, they'd been peeing in our garden—feral, mangy beasts who swarmed the city by the hundreds, surviving on scavenged chicken bones and bags of oily, discarded rice. My eight-year-old wanted war. When a hapless feline approached our sidewalk—intending to pee or not—David ambushed it with a stream of green pellets collected from beneath the olive trees down the block.

Toddling Adam and I joined him on the porch. "Want to walk a loop with us?" I asked. Together we stepped out for a walk around the block, David with his bucket of olives in tow. When we reached the top of the steep street parallel to ours, the boys dumped them on the asphalt, where they tumbled like tiny turtles or slow-motion marbles. David narrated their race like a sports announcer. Adam clapped his dimpled hands as he clomped down the hill in his moccasins, laughing and shrieking.

A shout interrupted our fun. "*Haram,* shame on you!" a boy scolded from behind his garden gate. "That's God's grace!"

Na'amat Allah—I'd heard this phrase applied to physical provision and blessings, any gift given by the Creator to mankind. In English, *na'ama* can be translated as *grace* or *favor*. I tucked the phrase into my mind, though a hunch told me this boy was being overly sensitive, parroting a criticism he'd heard from adults. He didn't know we'd gathered these olives off the sidewalk, hadn't wasted them by picking them off a tree.

I acknowledged the offended neighbor boy, then turned back to my sons. Adam's giggles spurred on David's sportscaster voice. I felt washed in delight. We chased our olives down the hill until their race puttered out, caught as they were by divots in the pavement.

* * *

I first explored the idea of na'ama in the context of bread. After a couple of years in Amman, it was clear to me that Arabs gave the foodstuff special treatment. Instead of throwing it away, they hung bags of stale *khubz* from trees near the sidewalk, where it grew green with mold. Snacking pedestrians didn't toss flour-based products in the garbage can; I'd seen last bites of falafel sandwiches moldering on walls, half-eaten cookies left on gateposts. Curious about this cultural phenomenon, I decided to write about bread.

Soon after moving to Jordan, my husband, Austin, declared himself a bread snob. He spent weeks questing after the perfect shop from which to buy our loaves. His search led him to the Oriental Bakery, an average establishment on a main road leading to the balad, Amman's original downtown. Their khubz was fantastic. They even made a whole-wheat version, which locals considered diabetic or dieting fare. Austin memorized the daily baking schedule, usually timing his shopping trips so he'd come home with chewy loaves that released steam when ripped open.

Of course, the owner of the Oriental Bakery seemed an ideal interviewee for the article I wanted to write. Zaher Jadallah received my request for an interview without fluster, as if it were completely normal for a foreigner to want to learn the details of mass-producing bread. Jadallah purchased the bakery a year and a half before our meeting, despite no background in baking. The business attracted him because in the Middle East, bread is one thing that keeps on selling. The Oriental Bakery produced about 2,860 pounds of bread every day, bought by residents of the surrounding neighborhoods, as well as nearby hospitals, hotels, and restaurants.

"Regular white bread takes less than an hour to make," Jadallah, a soft-spoken, middle-aged Jordanian, told me as we entered the bowels of the bakery. He pointed at different pieces of machinery in a high-ceilinged room. "The dough begins in the mixer and then moves to that machine, which portions it into balls and flattens them. Then they go on that belt to rise."

I held my notebook to my chest as I watched dozens of doughy rounds on their long, zigzag journey to the oven. After baking, the flatbreads cooled on a conveyor belt high above employees' heads before dropping into their ready hands. While it was still puffy and pliable, they stuffed the bread into plastic bags and laid them out for sale.

Though they aim to bake just the amount of bread that will sell in a day, the bakery always has a little extra. Jadallah pointed to an empty flour sack leaning against a wall—leftovers saved for shepherds who drive into Amman, trolling bakeries for cheap animal feed. Some customers use leftovers in creative side dishes like *fatet hummus* and *fattoush*.

"The most important blessing is bread," Jadallah told me as we sat in his office, a corner of the sales floor sectioned off with accordion panels. "Why? Because we can live on bread alone."

Jadallah believes all food is grace from God, as are blessings like physical health and children. For Muslims, stewarding these blessings is a religious concept, but the particular focus on bread is cultural. Islam does not command Muslims to pick up bread found in the street, kiss it, and put it on a high place, but these habits—which many Jordanians practice—developed as an expression of reverence toward bread.

Sujud, a friend from Syria's southernmost province of Dera'a, told me she gathers scraps of bread after meals and places them in a bag that never mixes with the rest of the garbage. When a family member takes the trash to the street, they hang it on the outside of the neighborhood dumpster. It's haram—religiously wrong—to throw away bread, she said, because bread is na'amat Allah. If you throw away blessings, God will not give you more.

"You're lessening your grace by your own hand," Sujud explained as we visited over glasses of tea. Her earrings, interlinking rings of gold, dangled on either side of her face. "God is not going to give to you because you threw away grace."

While we talked, our sons hollered in the next room, building forts with floor cushions and jumping from mattress to mattress with great energy. "When we're eating, my husband and I remind the boys not to put their feet on bread," Sujud continued. Having eaten meals with many Arab families, I could imagine Sujud, her husband, and their four boys sitting around a plastic cloth on the floor. In a set-up like this—with lively boys like these—stepping on bread was not out of the realm of possibility.

Before she and her family fled to Jordan as refugees, Sujud lived in a Syrian village where her mother owned twenty-five acres of land. As was common in Dera'a, they sowed their fields with chickpeas, lentils, barley, and wheat. Wheat harvest came in the summer, when the green fields ripened to gold. Every day her mother and grandmother made shraak, a very thin type of flatbread, often with flour milled from their own wheat.

"And what do Syrians do with old bread?" I asked.

"Every family in my village had chickens or pigeons, so we could feed them old bread instead of throwing it away," she answered. "Here in the city, the poor sometimes collect bags of bread to sell to shepherds or people with birds."

Ah, that's why I'd seen a veiled woman pulling bread from the dumpsters. That's why our neighborhood shepherd carried a bag of bread with him while herding his goats through traffic. That's why I'd once seen an old man pull a wad of dry bread from a bag, then wring it in his hands and sprinkle the crumbs on the wall for birds. The simple act looked holy to me—the act of someone trusting, knowing there would be grace for tomorrow, and that there was enough to share today.

* * *

Sometimes grace comes down in unexpected packaging, whetting not your palate but your soul.

For years, I'd been eyeing an enclosed yard on the corner near our apartment—a place I called the Secret Garden. While walking home from kindergarten with David, I'd crane my neck to peek over the wall topped with barbed wire, catching glimpses of color: drifts of white almond blossoms, clumps of miniature yellow daffodils, a patch of over-saturated red poppies so bright they looked electrified. On day twenty-three of the coronavirus quarantine, during a period when we were not supposed to leave our homes except for shopping, I tried to coax open the Secret Garden's gate.

Without warning, a stranger in the street called to me, a dark-skinned man with close-cropped, curly hair who dragged his right foot as he approached. I stepped away from the gate, acting like I hadn't been picking the lock.

"Do you need something?" I asked in Arabic.

"I live here," he answered.

Explanations tumbled from my mouth. "I was here earlier with my boys" (true—we'd even picked poppies from his yard), and "I just want to sit and enjoy the sun" (very true—lockdowns made me crave the open sky).

The man looked at me with eyes cloudy from premature disease. "Welcome," he said, opening the gate. "Please come in."

Right away my host asked, "Do you want to pick almonds?" The yard, which contained around a dozen small almond trees, would be a jackpot for Jordanians, who enjoy the immature green nuts as a spring snack. Kids and adults alike swarm urban almond trees each spring, climbing ladders, walls, and even rooftops to claw down the velvety green nuts. They eat them like candy—raw, crunchy, and tart—sometimes dipping them in salt for an added twist of flavor.

"No," I assured him, "I only want to sit." He returned to his apartment around the back of the one-story villa, leaving me to a trampled path through the tall grass.

Among the almond trees, I sat on the edge of a low stone structure, previously a fountain, now speckled with moss and lichen. Above my head were metal poles and wooden slats that once supported a grape arbor, and even higher, the branches of Aleppo pines overloaded with cones and a palm tree rattling dry fronds. On the other side of the wall, the street was silent, save the talk of pedestrians, about half of them wearing surgical masks. Bird song replaced car traffic in those days, so much so that sometimes we felt like we were living in a jungle with rock pigeons, laughing doves, alpine swifts, blackcaps, and white-spectacled bulbuls.

I inhaled the warm exhalations of plants, the soporific smell of chlorophyll. How good to sit quietly, away from David, who needed guidance through online school; away from Austin, who needed to figure out how to teach seminary courses over WhatsApp and Zoom; away from four-month-old Adam, who needed everything from me, the mama who couldn't even take him outside to pacify his grumpy moods.

I felt grounded by the green around me—the green I had dreamed of after our initial four days of lockdown in March 2020. Martial law had been imposed across the Kingdom, and we had not been allowed to step outside for ninety-six hours. The sky felt so generous on the fifth day—the day after the government failed to deliver bread to 10 million people's doorsteps, the day after Austin and I discussed who would get to drink the remaining milk in the refrigerator.

On the fifth day, I walked to the bakery and stood in line with a yard between me and my neighbors. After that, I'd gone for walks every day, scrounging for cans of tuna, bags of pasta, frozen hamburger patties at corner markets since full-sized grocery stores were shuttered. Every evening we sat down to dinner while Amman's repurposed bomb sirens announced the six o'clock curfew. We heard police cars chasing curfew-breakers and ambulances carrying emergency cases to the hospital. I ate and thought of my friends whose husbands were daily wage earners. Many nights I wanted to cry because I didn't know if they had money to buy bread.

It was all too much—but while I sat in the Secret Garden, I felt God laying a table for me in the wilderness of COVID-19 and newborn sleep, of unwanted responsibility and unwelcome restrictions. I could breathe here. I could lift my head and look the sky in its blue face. Grace—na'amat Allah—watered my soul as I experienced the simple gifts of breath, life, and freedom so pronounced.

When I stood to go, my host came down the path carrying a plastic chair. He'd cleaned up since we met; he now wore a long-sleeved sweater, scholarly spectacles, and striped, fingerless gloves. "Here is water," he said, offering me a bottle of water, "and these are for you." He held out a grocery bag half-full of furry green almonds.

"God bless your hands," I said, accepting the gift with a smile.

"Do you want coffee?" he asked.

"No, no," I said, inwardly swooning over his quintessential hospitality. "Thank you so much."

After I took an obligatory sit on the chair, during which the man withdrew to his apartment, I walked toward the gate. On the villa's back porch, a couple of shirts hung sloppily on a clothesline, and a pink geranium grew in an olive oil tin. I waved goodbye to my host. On my way back into our apartment building, I hung the bag of almonds on my neighbor's door handle, grateful to pass on a blessing.

* * *

A couple of times after moving to Jordan, I dreamed of my childhood olive tree. I'd wake with cobwebby memories of my sisters and I munching tangerines on the packed ground beneath its branches. With memories rekindled, my attention was captured each year by Jordanian farmers harvesting their olive trees throughout the country after the first autumn rain.

Wael Rabadi didn't bat an eyelash when I asked to interview him about olive farming. *"Ahlan wa sahlan,"* he told me warmly over WhatsApp. "You are most welcome." On a September evening, I sat in his home in central Amman, surrounded by bookshelves bulging with French and Arabic titles. Rabadi taught French literature at a Jordanian university and had met his wife in France during his years abroad. While their house cat wandered in and out and his son banged away at piano scales, Rabadi answered my questions about his farm in the northern city of Ajloun.

"We have a story about the olive tree," he said. "Once a king passed an old man planting an olive tree. 'Old man, you're about to die,' the king said. 'Why are you planting an olive tree? You won't eat from it.' The old man replied, 'They planted and we ate, so we'll plant so they'll eat.'"

Rabadi described how olive trees require very little water, how their roots stretch deep into Jordan's rocky, red soil and extract moisture lodged in the stones themselves. While the pastoral olive groves of the countryside attract more attention than city olives, Rabadi instructed me to notice the olive trees in Amman. Usually planted in the sidewalk and surrounded by concrete, these trees flourish in the midst of traffic, pedestrians, and air pollution, proving the olive's resilience and durability.

"The olive tree is mighty," Rabadi said near the end of our meeting. "It doesn't matter if you plow or don't plow, if you pull weeds or not." After feeding me homemade pastries stuffed with homegrown *za'atar*, an herb resembling oregano, we agreed to stay in touch so I could join him and his family at the farm during the harvest.

At the end of October, I sat cross-legged in Rabadi's olive grove, stripping ripe fruit from just-pruned branches. An American friend who'd connected me with Rabadi sat beside me. Her husband had his head in the tree with our industrious, bi-vocational host, who was dressed in cargo pants and a bucket hat.

"So you were raised on this property?" I asked Rabadi, motioning around us. Sixty mature trees and fifty smaller ones were planted on the two-and-a-half-acre plot.

Rabadi stepped out of the tree he was pruning. "I was raised under the trees," he declared with a grin. Although he'd only recently returned to farming after a long stint in Europe, Rabadi obviously relished the work and cultural traditions linked with it. He told us how historically, when olive oil production was the foundation of Jordan's economy, men would sleep in the fields to protect their crop from thieves. Sunrise would find them in the trees, picking and pruning dry or weak branches. The women eventually joined them with breakfast, then sat on the ground to pluck olives from the trimmed boughs.

Rabadi's grandfather had exchanged olive oil for his annual supply of sugar, tea, coffee, cardamon, rice, and cigarettes. His grandmother used oil to keep her skin soft and youthful, and his father would drink some every day for its health benefits. Rabadi remembers how, as a boy, his family would sell oil to buy bread, eggs, and schoolbooks.

"In the past, everything waited for the olives," he said. "The wedding waited for the olives, the engagement waited for the olives, buying clothes and shoes waited for the olives."

After about five hours of picking, during which we harvested two trees, we ate the lunch Rabadi's wife had prepared—a true French-Arab fusion with chicken, potatoes, and carrots stewed in herbs de Provence and green olives. On the kitchen counter sat a couple of big jars of table olives. The family had almost exhausted their annual supply, but now they would make more—piercing the fruits individually, then curing them for a couple of weeks.

Before leaving the farm with its view of Ajloun's twelfth-century castle, I gifted Rabadi with a copy of the novel *Gate of the Sun* by Lebanese author Elias Khoury. Olive trees almost act as characters in this dense tangle of Palestinian stories. They provide shelter to families fleeing Jewish militias, and an ancient tree serves as refuge for Yunes, a vigilante who secretly passes between Lebanon and his former village in northern Galilee. Khoury quotes this arresting passage from the Qur'an's Surah an-Noor, pure poetry in Arthur J. Arberry's interpretation:

> God is the Light of the heavens and the earth;
> the likeness of His Light is as a niche wherein a lamp
> (the lamp in a glass, the glass as it were a glittering star)
> kindled from a Blessed Tree,
> an olive that is neither of the East nor of the West

whose oil wellnigh would shine, even if no fire touched it;
Light upon Light;
(God guides to His Light whom He will).

A blessed tree—that was how Rabadi described olives too. *Holy* was another adjective he used. Consecrated organisms they seemed, common yet also set apart, revered. A member of a historically Christian tribe, Rabadi recalled how, before electricity, Jordanian Christians contributed portions of their olive oil to fuel the lamps in their churches, generating a smoky light.

Months later, Christ's words in the Gospels came to me: "I am the light of the world." Elsewhere he claimed to be the bread of life. To his Middle Eastern audience, these assertions would have held weight, a weight I felt as I researched. Was the Messiah in part making these bold declarations: *I am the most holy things, the grace and favor of God. I am his generous heart made flesh.*

* * *

Hospitality here is always extravagant, and food is inextricably linked with hospitality. When I started researching, I knew bread and olives were gastronomic expressions of Jordanian culture. But they're not just that. These foods are symbols of Arab cultural values, many of which are rooted in nomadic tradition evident millennia before Christ, in the stories of tent-dwellers such as Abraham, Isaac, and Jacob.

For centuries, nomadic Bedouin inhabited the Middle East—Jordan included—living in tents and moving with their herds of camels, sheep, and goats to find pasture. Hospitality was paramount to survival. When a visitor arrived from across desolate stretches of empty land, honor bound the host to receive and nourish him. Coffee and bread, a slaughtered sheep, a place to shelter from sun and wind—generous provision reflected honor back on the host.

In particular, tribal leaders called *shaykhs* were expected to provide for and entertain guests. I read of Mithqal al-Faiz, a prominent Jordanian shaykh who spent a full tenth of his monthly income on coffee. But in Inea Bushnaq's collection of Arab folktales, the Palestinian-American writer and translator considers generosity a hallmark characteristic of any nomad: "A man's worth is counted not so much by what he owns himself as by what he gives to others. . . . If his guests walk away praising his openhandedness, then he feels wealthy indeed, even if he and his family are reduced to feeding on milk and a handful of dates."

Though just a tiny percentage of the Middle East's population remains nomadic, this same generosity and consequent honor infuse Jordan's culture of hospitality. When my parents visited, our downstairs neighbor insisted on inviting them for mansaf, Jordan's national dish. We gathered in their living room around an enormous tray filled with al dente rice and steaming hunks of lamb. Um Husam distributed individual dishes of rice, then hand-selected pieces of meat for my dad and spooned tart yogurt sauce over my mom's rice.

A similar feast welcomed Austin's parents when they visited from Arizona. "Come Friday morning for a simple breakfast," our landlord's wife invited. When we settled into chairs on their covered patio, my in-laws couldn't believe the giant bowls of hummus and *foul* the family brought out, the fresh bread and the tea. They still talk about that breakfast, which is part of the point: Arabs know that if they serve a good meal, they'll be praised at home and abroad.

Hospitality appears in smaller ways too, in cultural games that are always in play. Politeness requires that if eating in public, you must offer to share with anyone around you. Even taxi drivers expect you to offer a bite of your sandwich. Though they'll surely decline, you'll be considered stingy if you don't, and God forbid you'd be viewed as stingy. At the park, moms you don't know slip your kids bags of chips because they brought extra. When you buy a car or get a promotion or have a baby, you bring sweets to your coworkers, an invitation for them to celebrate with you. If you've come far to visit someone and stay late, they'll inevitably invite you to spent the night. "Sleep here!" they'll declare, using the imperative. The nursery gives a free hyacinth when you purchase three ranunculus—you leave smiling, shaking your head, wondering how these places keep their books balanced, their giving is so willy-nilly.

These cultural rituals spring from a firm belief that generosity given equals generosity received. Even those who have little seem not to worry about conserving their resources. Why? Because they trust reciprocity. They can be more generous than is practical or affordable because every member of their society is expected to give lavishly too.

In their forty years of wandering, the Israelites challenged the one who'd delivered them from slavery in Egypt. "Can God spread a table in the wilderness?" they asked. Their tone was testy, sarcastic, streaked with the rebelliousness that brought the LORD's judgment on them in the first place. Yes, God could, the Psalms and the Pentateuch assert, and yes, he did, raining down on them the grain of heaven.

The Qur'an's fifth chapter, Surah al-Ma'idah—translated "The Table" or "The Table Spread with Food"—recounts this story of the wandering Israelites, followed by a story of Jesus and his disciples. The disciples ask for a sign, ask if God is able to send down a "table" at Jesus' request. They want some proof, some assurance, that Jesus' words are truth. In response, Jesus prays, "Send down upon us a Table out of heaven, that shall be for us a festival, the first and the last of us, and a sign from Thee. And provide for us; Thou art the best of providers."

I wonder, does submitting to this truth, really embracing the reality of God as provider, enable my Arab neighbors to share bread? Do they realize that when they break bread, they image the God who sustains them? Do they recognize that when they give, they mirror the generous heart of the One who provides?

* * *

On a spring morning, Austin and I invited our boys on an expedition. "Let's go find the oldest trees in Jordan!" To spice up the deal, we brought David's friend along. With just a pin on a map, we piled into our Prius to find Roman olives, some of the oldest trees in the world. *Will I finally find an olive tree rivaling that of my childhood?* I wondered as we drove.

Northwest of Amman, olive trees fill much of the land between villages, testament to the fact that they cover 72 percent of Jordan's agricultural lands. Life moves at a slower pace in these villages. Everything is shorter than in the city, with cinderblock buildings just one or two stories tall. Behind hastily mortared walls—some adorned with mosaics or glittery paint—gardens burst with grape arbors and lemon, pomegranate, and fig trees. Geraniums planted in powdered milk tins brighten street-facing walls. In one village, a mosque's minaret is just a concrete pillar with loudspeakers strapped to it.

Between the small- and medium-sized trees outside, I spotted buildings warehousing olive oil presses. I remembered the heavy scent of olive tapenade in the press near Rabadi's grove, how machinery in the warehouse crushed the olives into thick, brown paste. Farmers sat at spigots with four-gallon tanks and plastic jerry cans, carefully filling them with yellow-green streams of oil.

Our car threads the main streets of multiple towns. The roads are lined with poultry shops where crated chickens await the chopping block, and open-faced bakeries where bread is piled on wooden tables accessible from the street. Coffee shops bear names such as Blak Dark Coffee and Mugshot Coffee, and giant Arabic coffee pots—the regional symbol of hospitality—tilt in the middle of traffic circles. Kids in school uniforms wander home eating chips, alongside old men wearing long dishdashas, sport coats, and checkered shemaghs.

We eventually turned off the winding road, obeying Google's sophisticated, classical Arabic commands. Massive olive trees began to appear. From the back seat, David and his friend started exclaiming.

"Woah, look at that one!"

"That's sooo big!"

Forget the pin—we parked and climbed out, unable to resist the pull of the grove around us. I glanced at a house nearby.

Seeing no one around, I shimmied down an embankment and walked among the well-spaced trees. Hospitality again—it's such a valued trait that trespassing on private property is largely a foreign concept.

I stood in front of a thick, gnarled Roman olive tree that perhaps had been growing since before Christ's birth. A ring of leafed branches crowned it, surrounding a bare place where all of us stood—three boys and two adults—once we hefted ourselves up. We couldn't stop exclaiming over the tree's size and age. A holy thing it seemed—sacred. In a world where hardly anything lives 2,000 years, this tree was not just living but continuing to produce fruit. Thousands of olives were ready to be shaken down, the distillation of a year's sun, rain, and heat.

I stood in the olive's widespread arms, receiving the moment as a gift—because that's what grace is, right? *God giving us a free gift we don't deserve.* I memorized that definition as a girl. And how should we accept gifts? With delight, with pleasure, with joy. I've found that if I receive one thing as gift, all becomes gift. Receiving the first gift plows my heart to receive more. And so my eyes take in the hillside across from me, filled with grasses and rocks and flowers, all of them shouting praise.

Here's a picture I see as I imagine all of this grace raining down. I'm sitting with one piece of bread in a desert, hungry. I accept it—bismillah—and suddenly a table appears before me, set with a glass of tea with mint. As I reach for it, a kettle appears, its tea bag twirling in the breeze. Then springs up bread baked with olive oil and za'atar, that most blessed of Middle Eastern marriages, and a bowl blossoming with crispy falafel.

"Thanks be to God," I murmur, and the more I say "yes," the more the feast grows: soft cheese drizzled with oil, glistening olives, sliced cucumbers and wedges of tomato, fried eggs and hummus, a dish of crumbly, chalky-sweet halva—grace multiplying, compounding, snowballing until I raise my eyes to the table's end and come eye-to-eye with him, the shaykh of shaykhs, Lord of the worlds, his face all smiles. (Even a smile is *sadaqa*—a benevolent act that garners eternal rewards for the giver—and his holds a gleam of eternity.) He's open-armed, relishing my enjoyment, wearing a dishdasha impossibly white.

"One hundred welcomes!" he booms, and a canopy unfurls overhead, shading me from the sun in this suddenly bursting, wonderful wilderness.

Wiping my stuffed mouth on my sleeve, I smile back and run like a kid to his embrace.

PART 3

Devotion

CHAPTER 10

Yet I Will Rejoice

The figs have budded here, swollen, tanned, and cracked sticky, and they sell them in foam boxes off the backs of trucks while the rising sun blazes a blinding strip of light down the wet asphalt and I return to Amman after school drop-off, passing goats and skinny horses subsisting on thistles in the wadi, a roiling patch of pigeons foraging on scattered bread, bowed olive branches begging for relief and whispering to me Habakkuk's prayer—a prayer surely prayed in autumn—when the prophet imagined it all gone: fig trees bare, grape vines stripped, sheep pens empty—and yet he said he would rejoice in God—rejoice!—which makes me wonder about Habakkuk while walking past a grape arbor with clusters covered in paper bags, lantern-like, wonder what clear vision of God and his coming kingdom enabled him to rejoice in the face of food scarcity and injustice, and

I ask myself whether I have the grit to rejoice in the unseen when the seen contradicts it so convincingly—headlines about stalled Ukrainian grain shipments, a boat carrying refugees sinking off the Turkish coast, Jordanian unemployment cresting 25 percent—and I try to practice rejoicing but sometimes I don't know how, like when clutching the phone in front of a barred prison window (tell me—how do I rejoice then, when my deepest, rawest self laments?) or when I sit with a friend whose children defend her from her husband's blows or with a woman whose daughters face harassment because of their brother's shame, and I feel what foolishness, what naïve stupidity it is to rejoice, rather than to distract myself or medicate my unbelief with sleep, but I want to learn to rejoice like that, to hope in love when the world is on fire, to turn from the devastated, pain-wracked world and sit quietly with the one core truth of the universe—*chesed*—that recklessly loyal lovingkindness that made Habakkuk climb his watchtower searching, so teach me, teach me to rejoice when beggars knock because I still have food to give, to rejoice when anxiety cripples me claustrophobic because I will soon be redeemed, to lament when earthquakes hurtle rubble down—yes—but then to rejoice because restoration is on its way, to lament and rejoice now, even now, as I sit with a woman consumed by cancer, because the husk of her body, like a pomegranate, hides searing-red coals of promise, a trillion cells straining toward eternity.

CHAPTER 11

On the Border

I'm sitting in a tent on the Jordanian-Syrian border, translating for an American doctor who does not yet trust me. Her name is Holly. She wears powder-blue scrubs and running shoes and has blonde hair tied back with a scrunchie. Her face is all sharp lines.

The moment she saw me back in Amman—judged I wasn't Arab and probably guessed me a decade younger than I am—she told the Egyptian interpreter beside me that we needed more native-speaker translators. Today *is* my first day translating, which I do not tell Holly, but first days have to happen. And today she can't do her job without me.

"Can you ask her to take this off?" Holly tells me. "I can't take her blood pressure with the sleeve tight on her arm like that."

"Can you take this off?" I ask our middle-aged patient from Damascus. I'm careful to use the correct verb in Arabic—*to undress* rather than *to remove*. The woman peels the abaya from her arm and shoulder, revealing a flowered nightgown. Holly

145

wraps a cuff around her arm, filters out sounds of wind and children, and listens.

When the NGO I volunteer with asked if I could interpret today, they said we'd be going to a refugee camp near Mafraq, one of Jordan's northern border cities. Not the Za'atari camp, home to around 80,000 Syrians, but a small camp "on the border." I honestly don't know how close we are to the border or the name of the camp we're in. But I do know there are twenty-five children and their mothers sitting around us, and that outside a dust storm has engulfed the camp.

The tent we're in—striped red, green, and yellow on the inside—seems sturdy enough, but wind is bearing down on us. We need ventilation, so the flaps covering the tent's mesh windows are untied. Loose pieces of fabric flap and clang on the tent poles. A blue flowered carpet covers the ground of our pop-up clinic, lit by bulbs hanging from a cord looped around the central roof pole.

Holly removes the blood pressure cuff from the woman's arm, then listens to her lungs. She asks more about her symptoms before diagnosing her with pneumonia. I take a stab at pneumonia, guessing it *lung infection*. Holly writes a prescription for antibiotics, and we send the woman to our pharmacy, a set of tables six feet away, near where the Egyptian interpreter sits with a nurse practitioner.

A young mother wearing a pink floral headscarf sits down, tells us her name and age (twenty-four), and says she's taking birth control pills but still has period-like bleeding at times. Holly wants to know how many children she already has, and when she hears the answer (six), she's surprised. I have ceased to be surprised by numbers like these and the ensuing calculations of teenage marriage, though I do thank goodness I learned the clinical expression for *birth control pill* last week.

An American friend who works as a doctor in Amman teaches me all kinds of medical phraseology. He has misgivings about partnering with short-term teams like this, groups that fly in for a week or two, do their good deeds, and then leave without the ability to follow up with complex cases. He prefers to treat people directly, without interpreters. He'd rather not risk shaming the visiting doctor in front of a patient if he disagrees with her diagnosis.

"Explain to her there are two kinds of birth control," Holly says, "one that makes your period go away completely and one that doesn't. And she has to take it every day at the same time if she wants it to work."

I start in. "There are two kinds of pills," I say. "One that . . ."

A woman in black approaches and sits next to us. She listens to me for a few seconds, then slouches toward the young mom and talks under her breath. The young mom's eyes dart between me and her, and I catch the older woman's meaning: How can you ask about such a trivial matter when there are sick people waiting?

I've lost the young mom's attention.

"We want to see you," I tell the other woman with a manufactured smile, "but you will need to wait your turn." *Don't shame her,* I think. *Don't make a scene.* She shoots a few more comments to the young mom, mostly words I don't understand. I hear the verb *control*, and suddenly the young mom stands up and walks away. The woman in black slips into her chair.

"What just happened?" Holly asks. "Where did she go?"

I realize I haven't translated anything—words, body language, or insinuations.

"I think she just kicked her out," I say. An older woman in line tells me the woman in black is very sick, which justifies her cutting in line like that. Everyone stares as I follow the young mom and tell her to come back. "This can't happen," I say to the woman in black. "You must wait your turn."

Once we finish our birth control explanation, I take a sip of water and call our next patient. Her name is Khadija. Holly can't hear the heavy *kha*, doesn't know this is the name of the prophet Mohammad's first wife. She marks her down as *Ha*.

While we ask basic questions, a photographer circles. I tug at my headscarf and try not to feel self-conscious. It feels wrong—a man in a tent full of women, taking pictures of people who are unwell. He began taking photos the minute we climbed off the bus—lined up a few women, threw in a doctor and a translator, and took their picture before names were exchanged or basic information shared. I think of forms I signed when I started volunteering, about not taking pictures that could compromise the dignity of these refugees. I think of forms I signed when working with refugees in the United States. *This is not a field trip*, I think. *This is their life.*

Rain has started to patter on the clinic.

The woman in black has returned. I welcome her, apologize, try to make her feel comfortable. Compared to the other women her age, she is very thin. She tells us she went to the hospital a couple of days before, got IV fluids. She has pain in her stomach and back.

"Does her urine have a bad smell?" Holly asks. The answer comes. *Yes.*

"Ask her if it hurts when she has sex."

I pause, collect the sentence in my mind, then back up. "Are you married?" I ask.

"I'm a widow," she replies.

"She's a widow," I tell the doctor in English.

Holly meets my eyes with a half-smile. "Well, I guess that's the end of the conversation?"

"Yes," I say, relieved she understands. She prescribes antibiotics for a urinary tract infection and tells the woman in black to drink more water.

Rain drums on the tent. The nurses at the pharmacy pack away the medications, dozens of small boxes, wiping the fine film that's settled on them. The pharmacist has dusty shoulders. One of the guys who came with us to haul supplies looks like he powdered his hair. It stands up stiff.

I ask the Egyptian interpreter how to say pneumonia. "Infection of the lungs," she replies. Inwardly I cheer. *Just a few letters off.*

As everyone loads into the bus, I walk a few meters into the camp, tip-toeing through the mud. Standing on a rock in a clearing, I see four outhouses on the camp's edges, like points on a compass. There are about twenty UNHCR-issued tents, a pen of goats, a patch of zinnias. Someone said the owner of the olive grove next door employs the refugees.

"Are you finished?" a woman calls to me, breaking the post-storm quiet.

"Come!" I wave her over, and she picks her way across the mud with her daughter in hand.

She wanted her girl to see the doctor, she explains, but she was waiting out the storm. She's coughing and has a runny nose and sometimes a fever. I tell her it's probably allergies, that we didn't bring any allergy medication for kids. I think of my son in Amman, how he has the same symptoms as all these children, even without the ridiculous dust and lack of indoor plumbing. I imagine how his coughing would keep me awake at night if I didn't give him liquid allergy medication, if I had to sleep next to him on a mattress on the ground.

One of the American nurses approaches, and, without waiting for a pause in the conversation, tries to put a resealable plastic bag in my hand. There's a white bun with eggs inside, wrapped in a napkin, squirreled away from her hotel's breakfast buffet. It's been sitting in her purse for eight hours.

I know what the nurse wants me to do, and I don't want to do it. So the nurse gives the refugee her sandwich directly. The mother from Damascus says thank you, as she would no matter how she felt.

"*Tfuddalu*," she tells me, "Please, come visit us."

"Inshallah," I reply, which literally means, "God willing," but in this context means, "I'm sorry, I can't."

I turn to the bus and climb on, my sandals heavy with mud. The camp's leader, a middle-aged man in a long brown dishdasha and red-and-white checkered headscarf, waves us goodbye. The sky lies on the ground around him in a hundred blue-white shards.

CHAPTER 12

Sketches of Syrian Women

Every Syrian has a hundred stories in his heart.
Every Syrian is himself a story.

—Talia, TV correspondent from Aleppo

Hiba and I sit cross-legged on the carpet, the room around us quiet as her toddler sleeps. Sunlight stains the curtains brighter and brighter washes of yellow. "You were very sick, right?" she asks, bringing up an old conversation. "Tell me what was wrong."

Over the rim of my coffee cup, I look at Hiba—her head and shoulders swathed in a flowered scarf, pajamas stretching over her growing belly. Her skin is pale, her lips dry and cracked from the congestion that comes with her pregnancies. Her irises are so dark you can't tell them from her pupils; her short eyelashes do nothing to detract from her gaze. She stares this way at anyone, male or female, demanding answers.

I've known Hiba long enough that I answer her question freely, summarizing my year-long mental health battle and mentioning a few of its causes. When I finish my story, Hiba says, "You've hardly seen anything."

"I haven't even started to tell you what I've seen," I reply.

"Foreigners are so sensitive," she continues. "We even have a saying about it. 'If a foreigner gets spanked, he goes to the corner and cries, but if an Arab gets spanked, he hits his mama back.'"

Hiba is from Homs, a city decimated during the Syrian civil war that began in 2011. She saw people die in front of her and escaped under the Assad regime's shelling. I have experienced trauma vicariously, but my friend has faced terror and displacement firsthand, in ways I probably never will.

"Learn from us," Hiba says. "We have seen all these things, and we are still smiling."

* * *

The Jordanian NGO I volunteer with offers free medical care for refugees, as well as basic material support for new arrivals. I'm on the home-visit team, which exposes me to dozens of Syrian and Iraqi families. On these visits, we're able to provide companionship to people who are often lonely and disconnected, while assessing their physical, emotional, and psychological needs.

When I finish a day of home visits, I sit on the comfy, American-style couch in our living room—so big it could house a Syrian family. I brew a cup of anise tea (they say it quiets the nerves) and open my journal. I force myself to write the names of the individuals I met and where they were from, and if I have energy, bits of our conversations, descriptions of their apartments. "You have to move through the pain," a therapist once told me, and so I write—a simple way of memorializing people's stories and releasing some of the pain their stories bring me.

If I don't want to write, I knit like a fiend. This way I can forget everything—talk of bombs and strange, trauma-induced illnesses; the feel of a thin cushion on the floor beneath me; the thought of someone who didn't serve tea because she couldn't afford to buy tea. When I knit, I forget Arabic and focus on the language of stitches and rows in my hands. I try to pray, stitching images and stories into my work as if in so doing, I might redeem the pain of the world.

"Tell me what happened," Hiba said. What happened is difficult to condense, hard to explain to someone from a culture less familiar than mine with psychological terms and diagnoses. If my Arabic feels weak or I don't want to be vulnerable, I simply say I was very ill. Sometimes, mostly to Westerners, I say I had PTSD mixed with burnout and compassion fatigue. Sometimes I list the flood of symptoms I experienced: depression, insomnia, flashbacks, adrenal fatigue, panic attacks, a high startle response.

The basic facts are these: I've spent several years volunteering among refugees—first with Burmese immigrants in the Chicago suburbs, then with Syrians and Iraqis in Jordan. (More than a million Syrian refugees live in Jordan, a country of about 11 million.) I've been entangled in the world's largest post-World War II refugee crisis since before people started calling it that. I have burned out more than once. And though I've recovered from these periods of emotional exhaustion, I regularly find myself slipping into the fatigue that comes from being spread among too many needy people.

Maybe Hiba is right. Foreigners are sensitive—at least *I* am. Why I keep doing this, why I choose this work, sometimes I don't know.

* * *

Rana comes from the countryside east of Damascus. Her voice lilts upward at the end of her sentences like actresses in Syrian sitcoms. She smiles easily but often covers her mouth, conscious of the decay eroding her top teeth.

"Have you decided yet if you're going to return?" I ask one day.

"No, not yet," she says. "We might wait until school is finished."

For months, Rana and her husband have been talking about returning to Syria. Her parents never left, and his went back recently. Seven years after the civil war began, the situation is stable in Damascus. Schools and shops and hospitals are open. Because Rana's husband is too old to be drafted by the army and because her son is only four, they can entertain the option of returning. Many displaced families can't. They fear the regime will forcibly conscript husbands and sons of military age, and everyone knows that means possible disappearance, imprisonment, torture, or death.

Rana converses openly, surrounded by her brood of children. Here in Jordan, life is not easy, she explains. They get a little aid from the UNHCR or from a charity here and there. Her husband, who was a farmer in Syria, works as a tailor now, thanks to the Jordanian government's decision to grant work permits to

Syrians. But they don't have enough money to treat her thyroid problem, which visibly swells her neck. They can't afford to buy prenatal vitamins, though she's pregnant with their seventh child.

"At least in Syria, we wouldn't have to pay rent," she tells me.

Often Rana texts me with questions, floundering as she tries to care for her family's needs. *Do you know of a dentist? Can you help me sell my refrigerator? I have a request. Do you know anyone who could donate clothes for the baby?* I open her messages with deep breaths, my stomach sinking. Her needs flay me to the bone, exposing my limitations. Over and over, I'm shocked by how unconnected she is, by how little she knows of the world.

Partly, her husband is to blame. I've never met him, but I know he does not let Rana leave the apartment without him, except to visit one or two neighbors, women he has approved. She can't go to the market by herself or out for a walk. One time she told me she hadn't left the apartment in a month. She sets her phone on a windowsill in the sitting room, trying to catch a better signal.

I ask her, "But is he good to you at home?"

"Yes," she says. "This is just the way our men are."

* * *

Culturally speaking, "taking a walk" is not a common activity in this part of Amman, not for a woman alone. When I first moved here, I tried to follow local ideas of what a woman should be, so I only walked by myself if I had a destination. Since my recovery from PTSD, though, I take walks. "Exercise is the best medicine for anxiety," doctors and counselors all say, so I put in my headphones and zigzag our neighborhood's parallel streets, sweating beneath layers of clothes.

When I walk, I try to escape relentless, looping thought patterns and pay attention to details around me. I pause at forsythia cascading over someone's wall, an explosion of bougainvillea that literally forces me off the sidewalk. In an alley, I notice trees thick with green lemons and oranges. Depending on the season, I pick my way around olives smashed on the sidewalk or figs or a stone fruit Jordanians call "the most delicious in the world."

Near the traffic circle around which our neighborhood orbits, I glimpse the eastern half of the city, stone buildings stacked on hills for miles. At least half of Amman's population of around four million are immigrants, foreign workers, and refugees—Palestinians, Iraqis, Sudanese, Syrians, Yemenis, Egyptians. When I think about my childhood in a rural California community, where everyone was white and no one seemed poor, it's a wonder I'm here.

I trace back to the basic fact that brought me here: I live compelled by the love of a God I've believed in since childhood. Though I've faced evil and injustice in disadvantaged communities, I believe he loves the widow, the orphan, and the refugee, that he longs to see them treated with justice and mercy. I believe he's present and working among them, that I'm called to image and imitate him.

I'm very much a product of my generation's evangelicalism. I was a twenty-something who threw myself into social justice causes and radical Christian living. Now I'm a thirty-something who physically and psychologically suffered the consequences of unsustainable living yet still smolders with the philosophies that drove me to burnout. I know viscerally that social justice cannot save the world, but sometimes I still scramble around trying to find solutions to everyone's problems.

More than once this year, I've copied words from the prophet Zephaniah into my journal. *Fear not, let not your hands grow weak. The LORD your God is among you, he is mighty to save.* I read these words and tell my heart to be still, even though every household I visit leaves its mark on me. I remind myself that God is present. I remind myself that I'm not the savior.

On my walks around our neighborhood, I repeat Zephaniah's words, trying to believe them. I press my headphones in and let my music exegete the world.

* * *

Like Hiba, Muna is from Homs, formerly the third largest city in Syria. The first time I meet her, she is pregnant, full-term, carrying a baby without a brain. A doctor friend of mine had visited Muna's husband but didn't get to examine her because she stayed in the bedroom, sequestered from the eyes of non-relative men. This time he brought me with him to investigate.

Muna sits in her bed under a blanket, her tiny body wrapped in a flowered robe. Her dark hair, dyed bleach-blonde, is tied back with an enormous ruffled scrunchie. I sit on the bed with her, making small talk. She studied French in university before she and her family fled Syria. They spent a couple of months in the Azraq camp in eastern Jordan, where she met her husband while working for the same NGO.

I ask about the baby. She tells me they didn't discover its deformity until a prenatal check at seven months. He moves some, she says, but they aren't normal movements, more like shudders. She feels scared of whatever is to come. I lay my hand on her belly and pray for her peace.

A few days later, after delivering her son, Muna texts me.

> *I just wanted to tell you*
> *That I delivered and the baby died*
> *This is what our Lord wrote for me*

When was he born?

> *He was born on Saturday*

Did you see him?
Did you hold him?

> *Yes, we brought him with us from the hospital*
> *And brought him to the house*
> *And he died with us*
> *But he didn't nurse from me*

How many hours did he live?
Did you give him a name?

> *Fifteen hours*
> *Yes, we named him*
> *He came deformed*
> *But his face was so, so beautiful*
> *Our Lord made him so beautiful*
> *God have mercy on him*

Muna's Palestinian neighbors donate space in their family plot for the baby's burial, but Muna and her husband must rely on donations to cover the hospital delivery expenses. When I tell a fellow volunteer about Muna's situation, he gives me a tidy solution: "You should have prayed for healing."

* * *

A close friend recently made this observation about me: "It's like you continually have people in front of your eyes, like they never leave your consciousness." My friend is a task-oriented person, motivated by lists and efficiency and accomplishment. He has the skill of ignoring text messages and forgetting people if he's in a busy season at work.

If he could look in my head, my friend would see that my brain functions like an old-fashioned projector reel. Each refugee woman I know is contained on a tiny square of film in a white cardboard frame. These women project on my mind's eye continually; I tick through faces all day. *I haven't checked on her in a few weeks. I wonder how her family is handling the weather. I should visit her. I hope she doesn't feel forgotten.* Once I send a text or make a visit, I feel the pressure lessen as that woman's slide moves out of sight. But she's never discarded. Her picture just moves to the back of the wheel.

Sometimes I wish I could throw slides away. I want empty slots in my projector so my chest will not feel crushed. I want to forget Tamara, an artist whose husband abandoned her with six children, the youngest mentally disabled as a result of the bombing they experienced in Syria. I want to discard Maryam, who has to send her fifteen-year-old son to work in a factory because her husband had a heart attack and can't work anymore, and Ibtisam, whose husband went ahead of her to Germany, leaving her to wait here with two small kids. But I can't forget them. I feel unable, so marked am I by their stories.

While I'm inundated with Syrian families, a movie comes out called *A Private War*. It tells the story of Marie Colvin, an American journalist who worked as a war reporter for Britain's *Sunday Times* and died on the job in Homs in 2012. I do not watch the film—it's PG-13 and I'm too sensitive—but instead I read the *Vanity Fair* article that inspired the movie. I find in Colvin, who also had PTSD, someone who speaks my language. "I would like to have a saner life," she told someone shortly before her death. "I just don't know how."

I don't know how either—don't know how to forget, how to slow down, how to cease my striving and rest from my obsessive care for others. I don't know how, but I'm desperate to learn before another mental health crisis derails me.

I draw near to listen to these words from the prophet Isaiah: *In repentance and rest is your salvation,* he says. *In quietness and trust is your strength.*

These are not principles the social justice movement taught me, back when I first dove into volunteer work with trafficked women and addicts, refugees and immigrants. Rest and trust, the cessation of activity, the humble acknowledgment that I am small and inconsequential. My instinct rears against these characteristics, so counterintuitive when butted up against tremendous physical needs.

Isaiah, I argue, *how can I rest when I'm addicted to the adrenaline highs produced by operating in my second language?*

How can I still the frenetic pace at which I initiate, reach out, and check in on people? How can I trust when, really, I want to be someone useful and important and known?

Isaiah rebukes from the page: *You are not willing.*

Though his accusation couldn't be more apt, I walk away feeling ashamed, exposed.

* * *

Abeer is from Dera'a, the southwestern province of Syria where the revolution began in 2011. I met her on a winter afternoon when my ear was not yet tuned to the Syrian dialects. I kept my coat on, and we sat next to each other in the light from the open front door, eating clementines and drinking tea so sweet it made my teeth hurt.

I don't see Abeer again until nine months later, a gap for which I frequently felt guilty. I find the family's new apartment at the end of a few narrow alleyways. After we settle on the floor cushions in her living room, I ask why they moved.

They moved a month or two before, she informs me, because her elementary school-aged son, Ziad, had been violently assaulted by two teenagers. Ziad had gone missing for hours, only to return with Abeer's husband in the middle of the night, bleeding.

My eyes don't leave Abeer as she speaks. A pigeon-gray headscarf frames her fine-lined face. She controls her voice well but stares at me with shock, still not able to digest what happened. As news of Ziad's assault spreads through their extended family, people speculate and gossip, blaming what happened on Abeer.

"This is not your fault," I counter. "This is not your fault."

In the days that follow, I sort through memories, trying to place Ziad's assault on the scale of awful stories I've heard. It ranks very high. I review the story's key verbs—words I learned in Arabic class and hoped never to use, words I told Abeer I would not share with anyone.

I become Abeer in her pain, raw and numb. I've experienced this before, empathizing to the point where I have a hard time distinguishing my inner life from someone else's. I become blind to goodness or hope in my own circumstances as I live another person's reality. This innate, deep capacity for empathy has damaged me before. I know that healing will require me to disengage for a time, to separate myself from Abeer so I can become myself again. Unfortunately, applying this knowledge is tricky.

Since that visit, I've had insomnia most nights. Sometimes I wake up in a panic from a stressful dream. I'm wandering alleyways in Amman, trying to find a refugee family's apartment. I'm with Abeer and Ziad, trying to get somewhere. I see faces shrouded in black *niqabs*.

The psychiatrist tells me I'm too responsible. He circles a word on a graph in his file, a word that's soaring above the baseline. *Responsibility.* Then he draws a line from that word to one that's plunged beneath the line. *Self-care.* We talk about medication, whether I should go back on an antidepressant. We resolve to wait a little longer, to first try counseling and a break from refugee work.

In this season, I consider Hiba's words to me: *Foreigners are so sensitive.* I feel defensive. How light I'd feel if I were her, if the only expectations I had for myself were to care for my children, cook a good meal every day, keep my house clean and laundry washed, make my husband happy. When she used that word, she may have meant *emotionally aware*, but I'm guessing she meant *weak*. And though I do cry at others' pain and grieve the wrongs of the world, I rebuff this idea of weakness. I would describe myself as overly burdened, carrying the stories of many, many people. Like it or not, I bear responsibility for others, feeling compelled to respond to their needs even when they are not mine to bear.

Some of this internal pressure comes from statistics. So few Westerners can speak Arabic. Even fewer actually live near refugees, and even fewer are women who can access the lives of Syrian women, so often cloistered by a segregated society. Statistically, I'm compelled to go to the front lines. Something Marie Colvin said of war reporters rings true: We must go in and bear witness to what we see.

This idea of bearing witness hooks me. Who will tell these women's stories if I don't? Who will visit them if I don't? Who will remind them that they are loved and not forgotten? Who will encourage and honor them with presence? I know what Isaiah told me—I should be quiet and wait for God to act. But when I don't see him responding, I wonder who *will* if I don't jump in head-first and get something done.

Sometimes I wonder if I'd still be in this work if I were not a person of faith, though my beliefs don't necessarily make my job easier. Even as I choose faith—hoping in what I cannot see—I don't often feel more stable as a result. God-sightings are so few that faith in his presence and justice sometimes feels untenable. Sometimes I feel foolish to believe; sometimes I feel like I'm walking on a spider's web of convictions that could dissolve at any time.

Fear not, Zephaniah reminds me, *the LORD is among you; he is mighty to save.* I tell women this—that they are not forsaken by God—and they nod their heads in agreement. We kneel and lift our hands in supplication. We pray for the war in Syria to end, for healing and provision for their families. We say *amin* and pass our hands over our faces. And we wait, some of us believing, some of us unsure that God can heal or save—or that he will.

* * *

This whole building—four floors loosely connected by blood and marriage—is inhabited by Syrians from the Raqqa Province, the area ISIS made their capital in Syria. When my doctor friend and I visit, representatives from each household filter down, bringing medical concerns. One of the men needs a cortisone shot in his knee. The toddler has sores on his scalp. Someone dumps a plastic bag of medications and medical reports at my friend's feet.

Rawan, the wife living in this ground floor apartment, welcomes everyone into the sitting room, where a sequined *shahada* hangs on the sponge-painted wall. *I confess there is no god but God, and Mohammad is the prophet of God.* Rawan is obviously in charge here—the *sheikha* of the house, we joke—with her loud voice, flashing smile, and easy laugh. Nadeema, much quieter than her cousin, sits next to me, wearing the brown and white polyester pullover hijab she wore last time I saw her. I ask how she is doing.

"*Alhamdulillah.* Thanks be to God."

I ask, what is her news.

"Alhamdulillah."

I ask, how is her baby.

"*Nizil*," she says. *He fell.*

Nadeema doesn't cry, but her eyes, set in a dark, wide face, get wet. She was six months pregnant; this is her tenth miscarriage in a row. She says she's weary from the loss of blood, describes how the room looks dim. "God have mercy on him," I say, which I'm sure is not what you say for an unborn fetus, but I don't know how else to reply. I grab her hand, think about how I put my palm on her belly two weeks ago and prayed for that child. What does it mean that I've prayed for two unborn babies this year and they've both died?

Part of me wants to linger in her grief, but from our corner, Nadeema and I are drawn into the jovial atmosphere of the room. The doctor prepares to give Nadeema's husband an injection—all the guys are teasing, cajoling him to be brave. Kids run in and out of the living room, resulting in multiple close calls with the open-flame kerosene heater where Rawan is brewing tea. She throws witty comments across the room, putting everyone in an uproar.

Over-caffeinated by coffee followed by tea, my senses are cranked up to 110 percent. I realize that moments like these—sitting knee-to-knee with suffering people who are still laughing—these are what keep me in this work. I think about my first refugee friends in the Chicago suburbs. When I spent time with them, I felt like I was being reborn, like I was discovering what God designed me to do. I feel that invigorating burst as I sit beside Nadeema.

Many people couldn't handle this environment, but I can. I can take the dissonance of moving through settings I do not fully understand. I can listen to refugee stories for hours. I can help in practical ways and then allow my hosts the reciprocity of giving in return. This work wounds, yes, but it brings healing too. In moments like these, we sit together, surrendered to the hard facts of life yet choosing to enjoy the grace of being alive.

The darkness outside Rawan's open window hums with the call to prayer. Contentment dawns—quietly, unannounced, like a desert sunrise. I return to Isaiah, ready to listen. This time he speaks a soothing promise: *The LORD longs to be gracious to you; he rises to show you compassion. For the LORD is a God of justice. Blessed are all who wait for him.*

Here's the comfort I seek while swamped with unsolvable problems in the lives of those around me—this knowledge that God loves me and longs for me though I'm at once feeble and rebellious, though I stand condemned by my exhausted efforts to please people and my thirst to find value and identity in serving others.

I begin to see Isaiah's vision with him: God in heaven and me on earth, him waiting for me to wait for him. God desiring to pour mercy on me, if I'd just sit still a minute. A fresh perspective on waiting crystalizes, the sense that God does not view it as waste but as worship.

* * *

When Rawan speaks, her voice sings. It slides up and down scales, modulates, bright and melodious. She sends brief, staccato messages, spurts that make little piles on my phone screen. Sometimes she starts talking before she presses *record*. Her husband's canaries chirp and trill in the background, her kids screech nearby. I can hear her smile—always this exuberant smile that makes sound lines dance and dive.

She radiates joy, and yet Rawan knows about suffering. She and her family fled Raqqa in 2014 after enduring soaring prices, one hour of electricity a day, and multiple bombardments that forced them to their neighbor's basement for shelter. When Rawan decided to leave Syria, she and her kids made it to the Jordanian border, only to sleep on the ground for seven nights while waiting for permission to cross. Once inside, they were transferred to a refugee camp, where her oldest daughter contracted a kidney infection from drinking the dirty, yellow water. After ten days, Rawan escaped the camp with her kids. In the desert, she found a car that took them to Amman.

In the city, she's lived in an apartment with interior walls that were so thin they'd sometimes get shocked by the electrical wiring. One night, the building's roof collapsed on their upstairs neighbor. Her kids are bullied because they're Syrian.

Her husband sat with us once when I came to visit—bald, wearing sweats and a T-shirt, leaning back on a pile of pillows. He mocked Rawan for being emotional when scrolling through her relatives' social media feeds. I prickled. Rawan remained silent, thin-lipped, as she chopped chicken livers and scraped them into a bowl.

"In our society," she tells me later, "the woman must endure much."

Resilience flickers in this woman like I've before witnessed. Though she has lived through and continues to live under strain and stress, she lives with constancy, courage, and grace, one among many who have suffered tremendously and still stand tall. She doesn't have a victim complex, doesn't use her suffering as an opportunity for self-promotion. She weeps because she misses her family, grieves that her kids can't be close to their grandmother. Her heart is sensitive but strong.

When I observe her, I'm able to reject the idea that sensitivity equals weakness. She makes me wonder if Western approaches to mental health can promote weakness. Are Westerners weakened by psychological labels and diagnoses? Are we crippled and inward-focused by our obsessive need to process? Are we really stronger and healthier, more able to face suffering and challenges as a result of all our therapy?

As far as I know, Rawan has never visited a therapist or read a self-help book, but she's not crushed by her circumstances, doesn't drown in traumatic memories, carries herself with dignity in her need. She accepts what God has written for her, thanks him regardless of her circumstances. At dawn she prays in the window-enclosed side room where the purple chiffon curtains rustle with angels.

Perhaps because of her adaptability, her rebellious joy, Rawan's house is rarely her own. She is magnetic; a tide of Syrian women wash in and out of her door. She's a refuge for Ayat, a girl married at age sixteen, illiterate, and unable to get pregnant. She welcomes Haifa, mother of only one child, who reminds me of a Dom woman with her colorful, spangled dresses. When Rahma and Nour and Amal visit, I hardly get a word in. I listen to their rowdy voices, their boisterous expressions. I relish the blessing of being privy to these kinds of meetings that only half the world can see, to participate in unguarded interactions reserved for women only. And I find in Rawan an example—a way I too can live sensitive and strong.

* * *

When Hiba delivers her baby, a son, I visit her and hold him for two hours. Yazin has his mama's eyes. He's bundled in blankets like a marshmallow, but when Hiba touches his nose, she says he's cold. We cocoon his head deeper in the blankets before drinking cinnamon and turmeric tea with walnuts and coconut floating on top.

At his two-week checkup, Hiba and her husband learn that Yazin has a heart problem. At a specialty hospital, they discover his aorta is pinched and narrow like a kinked hose—a rare condition requiring surgery. When he is thirty-three days old, Yazin fasts for hours before his operation.

I go to the hospital to sit with Hiba. When I open the door to their room, a woman I don't know glances up from the couch. "*As-salaamu aleikum*," I say.

"*Aleikum as-salaam*," she replies.

I step in and peek behind the gray curtains surrounding Yazin and Hiba's bed. "I'm looking for a Syrian woman," I explain.

The woman on the couch looks up from her phone. "I'm Syrian," she says, staring at me with light eyes.

"I mean my friend," I reply, "whose baby is having surgery."

"She'll be back soon," she tells me. "You can sit down."

Ghada is from Quneitra, a governate tucked in Syria's southwestern corner, near Lebanon and the Golan Heights. She and her family fled to Jordan in 2014. She's here today with her two-year-old daughter, who she brings to me after she wakes.

The minute I take Amal, I know I will love this child and be depleted by her. I know compassion will require my all. Ghada tells me she can't swallow regular food and can barely drink milk. Her arms and legs have no muscle tone; they feel like the limbs of a newborn or a starving child, all bones. From birth they could tell something was wrong with her, but this is the first time they've had the opportunity to come to the hospital.

After more than an hour, Hiba returns, and we chat while she pumps a bottle of milk to take to Yazin in the ICU. She's cheerful and energetic as she tells me she slept well last night and took two naps yesterday. Her mood makes me self-conscious and slightly annoyed. She isn't exhibiting the somber emotions I expect from a mom with a newborn about to have heart surgery. Is she just not capable of these? Has her past calloused her so much that she is incapable of vulnerability? Or is her trust in God bigger than mine?

We make our way downstairs, passing through the double doors leading to intensive care. In a glass-walled room, we stand near Yazin, who's propped up in a full-sized hospital bed, a blip in a sea of white sheets. Machines beep around him. A plastic oxygen tube comes out of his nose, and nurses have prepared an IV site on his one-month-old wrist. He is naked except for a blanket around his waist and legs.

"He's cold," Hiba exclaims after she leans in to kiss his fingers.

I stand back, letting my friend absorb her son's condition. I know I won't last much longer here, though Hiba's just returned.

With her characteristic force and energy, I know she'll urge me to stay, but I can already imagine collapsing in the back seat of a taxi and zoning out, letting my emotional tank refill.

When Hiba turns around, her eyes are full of tears. Something blinks inside me—I feel surprise, maybe, or wonder. An unexpected crack has opened in my friend. She is choosing to let me look deep inside of her. Part of me wants to respond perversely, to tell her, "I told you so. I told you this would be hard." Part of me wants to hold this over her—the day she couldn't hold it together. Just for a moment, I want to be stronger than her.

But in the same instant, I recognize that maybe my self-sufficient Hiba needs me, needs compassion and kindness today. I won't be snide, won't blockade myself in my weariness. Instead, I choose to open my arms and embrace her, channeling a mercy not my own.

CHAPTER 13

My Other Name Is Hagar

Hala named me during our first session as teacher and student. We'd previously interacted at the Arabic center; she was effervescent, spontaneous, and hilarious, qualities that led me to request her as my instructor. But like many Arabs, she could not pronounce my first name easily—the vowel and consonant blends were like gravel in her mouth.

In a tiny glass box of a classroom, Hala and I sat across from each other at a plastic table. "Hmm, what can we name you?" she thought out loud, tapping her pen on a notepad. Her nails were painted, lips plumped with lipstick, headscarf wrapped tight. She'd already opted out of calling me Hadeel, her sister's name, a name to which a couple of people had compared mine during my two years in Amman. "Hajar. How about Hajar?"

"Hajar," I repeated, leaning forward, watching her mouth shape the letters. A light *h* sound, an elongated *a*, a rolled *r*. "What does it mean?"

"It's an old name," she said glibly. "It's in an old song." With that, she wrote my new name at the top of her notepad and our lesson began.

* * *

Soon after I started introducing myself as Hajar, I realized it was the Arabic form of Hagar, a name that frankly sounds ugly in English. Perhaps the American comic strip "Hagar the Horrible" influenced me, Hagar being the name of a bungling, red-headed Viking.

More likely, my negative connotations about Hagar sprang from my religious tradition. Hagar was the servant of Sarah, Abraham's wife, the Egyptian woman who conceived and bore Ishmael who was not the true son of promise. My associations with Hagar had been further shaped by the Pauline passage that casts her as a woman bound by the law, a supreme anti-model for Christian believers.

I quickly discovered that some Jordanian Christian women shared these perceptions. I met a couple of them one day outside my apartment building. They had dyed hair, wore slacks and short-sleeved polyester blouses, and carried handbags on their shoulders.

"My name is Heather," I told them, "or Hajar in Arabic."

One woman crinkled her nose, a look of disgust crossing her face. "You don't want to be called that."

* * *

The reactions I received from Muslim women couldn't have been more different. The name endeared me to them, eliciting smiles and exclamations. "Hajar was the wife of our lord Abraham," they told me, using the title given to all honored prophets. "She had a son, Ismail, and when she was stranded in the desert, Allah rescued her."

As I listened to their commentary, I recognized their reverence for Hagar, which echoed Catholic respect for the Virgin Mary. To these women, my name carried weight, significance, import. I got the impression it was a name to be lived into. I felt a weight of responsibility. Who was this woman, and who should I be because I bore her name?

A Syrian friend and I sat in her living room one day, drinking coffee and eating small, tart apples. Our kids had abandoned us for better entertainment. From the open window where her planter boxes sat empty, soft blocks of sunlight entered, warming the short-pile carpet where we sat. The scent of incense lingered around us; she'd been starting her mornings with incense and a chanted chapter of the Qur'an.

I leaned forward, eager for more details about my namesake. "Tell me Hajar's story."

* * *

The Qur'an does not mention Hagar by name, though hadiths of the prophet Mohammad fill out her story. These records say that Allah told Ibrahim to take Hajar and Ismail to the area of Makkah and leave them there. Ibrahim obeyed God's instructions, leaving the nursing baby and his mother in the desert with a bag of dates and a skin of water. When Hajar saw that Ibrahim was abandoning them, she called after him, asking why. When he told her this was God's command, she submitted. "Allah will not neglect us," she said.

Soon the water Ibrahim left them ran out, and Hajar's milk supply dried. Under the beating sun, Ismail thrashed and wailed, then became listless from dehydration. Hajar could not bear to watch his agony, so she ran up a nearby mountain. On the top of as-Safa, she shaded her eyes, searching for Allah's deliverance. Then she tucked her robe into her belt and ran to al-Marwa, still looking, prayers on her parched lips.

She repeated this desperate, hopeful run seven times, and then she heard a voice. She looked to the place where she'd left Ismail and saw the angel Jibril digging in the sand. She ran down to join him. With her hands, she formed a basin to catch the water burbling from the ground. She satiated her thirst, then cradled her son to her breast and nursed him.

Today, the water that sprang up for Hajar is called Zamzam. When Muslims make their religious pilgrimage to Mecca, they don't just circumambulate the Kaaba, the black-shrouded shrine built by Ibrahim and Ismail, the place toward which Muslims worldwide turn when they pray. Pilgrims also drink the Zamzam water and walk between as-Safa and al-Marwa in an air-conditioned gallery. They remember the Qur'an's words that Ibrahim left Hajar and Ismail in the desert to "establish prayer." In these ways, Hajar's exile and expectant acts of trust are memorialized by millions year after year.

* * *

In spite of the respect with which Muslims view Hagar, I didn't meet an Arab with my name until I'd lived in Jordan more than six years. We had moved to a new area of Amman. Adam, my endlessly energetic toddler, and I took frequent walks around the neighborhood. He stumped along in his moccasins, and I followed, breathing fresh autumn air tinged with sun-ripened olives.

A couple of older apartment buildings sat behind ours. One had a grape arbor over the car port, creating a dappled rectangle of shade in which a few women often sat in the late mornings or early evenings. One day as I passed with Adam, one of them hurried out to meet me. She had a thin face, sun-spotted, with dark crescents under her eyes, and a cold sore in the corner of her mouth. Her black-and-white head covering was stretched out, exposing a couple inches of gray-laced hair. I asked her name.

"Hajar," she said.

My right hand slapped my chest involuntarily. "That's my name too!"

She smiled at me. "We are destined for each other."

* * *

Like Islamic traditions about Hagar, Jewish perceptions of her are more positive than Christian ones. My Israeli-American friend described her fascination with Hagar, how she sometimes wondered if the solution to the Palestinian-Israeli conflict was hidden in her story. She told me that a Jewish tradition identifies Hagar as an Egyptian princess. Indeed, according to Rashi's commentary on Genesis 16, Pharoah said, "Better for my daughter to be a maid in [Abraham's] home than a ruler in another."

Other midrashim—Jewish explanations of biblical texts—say that because Hagar was raised in Abraham and Sarah's tents, she was accustomed to seeing angels. An article on the Jewish

Women's Archive expands on this idea. "The rabbis also empha-size her ability to perceive and interact with divine messengers," writes Tamar Kadari, "demonstrating her spirituality and ability to connect with God." Some traditions even equate Hagar with Keturah, the wife Abraham took after Sarah's death. Accord-ing to this interpretation, Hagar remained chaste in the wilder-ness, refusing the touch of other men and eventually returning to Abraham pure.

* * *

A surprising amount of medieval and Renaissance artwork focuses on the moment Abraham sent Hagar and Ishmael out of his home. Some paintings show Hagar in red velvet, a siren who tempted Abraham into an ultimate act of unbelief. Many scenes include Sarah peering over Abraham's shoulder, vindictive and smugly pleased. Depictions of Hagar and Ishmael in the wilderness feature massively winged angels, lots of trees, and usually some kind of water jar.

A marble sculpture of Hagar by nineteenth-century artist Edmonia Lewis stands as a crisp contrast to these paintings. At a time when Egyptians were considered Black, it's curious that Lewis—herself of African and Indigenous American descent—portrayed Hagar as European, with a small mouth and nose and wavy hair flowing back over her shoulders.

But the other details Lewis carved present a convincing portrait of Sarah's slave. Hagar stands with face uplifted, hands loosely clasped in front of her. Her body appears to be in motion, or about to move—one foot lifted off the ground in readiness, her tunic flowing backward. She shows signs of hurried flight, with the shoulder of her dress ripped and one side of her skirt hitched up in her waistband. An overturned pitcher sits at her feet. The absence of Ishmael in Lewis's sculpture clearly indicates to me that she intended to depict Hagar's first meeting with God in the wilderness, as recorded in Genesis 16.

Lebanese Christian theologian Tony Maalouf spends considerable space exploring this portion of Hagar's story in his book, *Arabs in the Shadow of Israel*. In an ancient Near Eastern context, Hagar's pregnancy conferred upon her great honor. Though she was a slave, she had become a mother, something her elderly mistress had never experienced.

Maalouf helps modern, Western readers imagine the characters' evolving attitudes toward one another. Hagar, beginning to feel the privilege of her position, withholds some of her service to Sarah, throws condescending barbs when Abraham isn't present. Abraham, pleased and proud that he will finally have a child, starts to treat Hagar preferentially. Sarah, naturally, gets angry. Exasperated, Abraham tells Sarah she can do with Hagar as she wants, leading to Hagar's abuse and subsequent flight.

Maalouf says Hagar probably fled about sixty miles south of Hebron to a region called Kadesh, solidly in the modern Israeli Negev. She headed south, toward Egypt. *Did she think she would return to her home country?* I wonder. *How many months pregnant was she at this point? Did she flee Abraham's camp in the night? Did she pack any provisions for her journey?*

When she stopped at a spring near a place called Shur, Hagar was met by the angel of the LORD, who told her to return to Sarah and submit to her. But he didn't leave her without comfort, Maalouf notes. Rather, the angel delivered bolstering promises about the embryo in her womb, the developing seed wrecking her hormones. Though she was a slave, God would multiply her descendants. Her son would be "a wild donkey of a man." Quoting Shimon Bar-Efrat, Maalouf says this metaphor implies that "the son would be a free man, independent like the nomadic tribes of the desert, not a slave like his mother." Maalouf adds that the angel's promises sketch a man "who will be free and strong, able to fight against all who desire to subdue him and to preserve his freedom as a nomad."

Looking at Lewis's sculpture of Hagar, I see wonder on her face—wonder that the angel of the LORD calls her by name (notably, Sarah and Abraham never do in the Genesis account), wonder at the invigorating, sustaining promise of a free and mighty son. Solemn-faced, her brow slightly furrowed with trepidation and incomplete understanding, she is erect, focused, listening. The lifter of her head has spoken. *I must do this hard thing, but there is future hope,* she thinks. *I will obey because God sees me and my affliction, and because he has promised me good.*

In this annunciation-like moment, Hagar responded to the angel of the LORD, saying, "You are the God who sees me." Hagar became the first person in the biblical record to name God—she, a woman and a slave. I wonder how Hagar looked as she returned from this encounter. I create my own painting in my imagination, sculpt her in my mind's clay. Wrapped in a flapping cloak with embroidered edges, she crests the hill to Hebron. Abraham and Sarah spot her from afar. She returns their shocked gazes solidly. Returning to hardship, she stands tall and dignified, transformed by her encounter with a God who knows her.

* * *

A painting by French artist Jean-Charles Cazin depicts the second half of Hagar's story, recorded in Genesis 21. Wearing a neutral-colored linen headscarf, Hagar stands with her face in her hands, trying to hide her distress from Ishmael. He leans against her with his hands reaching up, lost in her scarf. He appears to be nine or ten years old, like my boy David, and he stares up at his mother, attuned to her emotions, looking to her for guidance. I recognize that Hagar is trying to be brave and hold it together, but deep shudders well up in her as the full weight of realization strikes her. *We have been rejected, stripped of our home and our security. We are lost.*

Cazin's landscape gives the sense that the pair have just reached the desert—the rise behind them shows the transition from forested hill to sand. White, cubic shapes on a distant slope suggest a settlement or a grouping of goat-hair tents. And yet, though the narrative mirrors that of Adam and Eve's expulsion from Eden, Cazin paints a hopeful paradox. Abraham and Sarah's distant home is shrouded in dim light under a clotted, stormy sky, but light shines brightly on the sand around Hagar and Ishmael. Here in a place of exile, yellow flowers grow, hardy glimpses of mercy. If Hagar can wipe her tears, she'll notice that a trickle of water has passed through here, raising tender herbs in its path. If she can find the courage to seek them, she'll find signs of God's love waiting.

In this way, Hagar's story bursts with application for me, for I live in a dry land not far from where she wandered. Like her, I'm a mother who has stood in the kitchen and cried, my boys peeking around the corner with concern. I've felt lonely, suffocated by the mind-numbing monotony and self-cancellation we call motherhood. I've wondered how I will care for my sons so far from family and my own language and culture.

Unlike Hagar, I have chosen to live here—I wasn't rejected by my community—but can we acknowledge the myriad forms a wilderness can take? I know women who *have* experienced rejection—a friend whose husband left her for another woman, a refugee whose spouse bailed to another country. I know women facing unjust treatment and unequal opportunity, women who have been ostracized from their communities. Women skirting the deserts of hunger, who knock on doors because they can't put food on the table. Women in valleys of grief as dark as a desert night without a moon. Women carrying the desert in their wombs.

I know so many Hagars. Aren't we all her in a way, voices howling into wastelands of depression, anxiety, abuse, loss, joblessness, illness, old age? Women calling out, "How long, O LORD? Will you forget us forever?"

* * *

Pakistani-American scholar Riffat Hassan describes Hagar as a woman marked by fortitude and resilience. She also notes that her name is loosely associated with the Arabic word for *hijrah*, which she defines as "going into exile for the sake of God."

"When one is in the wilderness," Hassan writes, "without the protection of any familiar framework or faces, one's faith in God and one self [*sic*] is put to the real test. Those who are willing to confront the challenge of hijrah, to leave their place of origin or sojourn in order to live in accordance with the will and pleasure of God, gain merit in the sight of God."

When I read this passage, I hear a tinkling bell of recognition. Isn't this what I've experienced while following God like a nomad, rootless in this world? Yes, the wilderness depletes me, pushes me to the edges of myself. But at the edges of myself, I'm pressed into God like a purifying mold. In dry places, he makes me a well-watered garden. Perhaps I'm like the Beguines, medieval European mystics who emphasized the centrality of suffering in knowing God and the desert as a place to encounter him.

Whoever I'm like—a Beguine or Hagar—if I'm going to survive here, I must doggedly pursue God. This is essential. I must run back and forth between desert mountains, seeking the One who sees me.

* * *

Christian theology calls the appearance of the angel of the LORD a theophany. The angel of the LORD is not just any angel; he is, in fact, the preincarnate Christ. So on a hot day in the shade of his tent, Abraham served bread and meat, curds and milk to three men, one of whom was Christ. Jacob wrestled with, had his hip dislocated by, and was renamed and blessed by Christ. Moses heard from the burning bush the voice of Christ. And in the wilderness, Hagar was met by Christ.

The God who sees me, Hagar called this angel. The one who saw her affliction and abuse was the One who would be afflicted—head circled with thorns, hands and feet pierced with nails—the One who will bear these signs of abuse for eternity.

The one who offered her comforting promises is the One in whom all the promises of God become "yes."

This realization illuminates me for days. Suddenly I have an answer for Arabs who ask me, "How can you live here?" Can I whisper to them this secret, this mystery I've experienced for years but can just now articulate? *I have found a spring of living water that never dries, never stops flowing, more constant and eternal than Zamzam.* Will this answer silence and satisfy them? *Just as Christ met Hagar in the desert, so Christ meets me here.*

The wilderness is full of this Christ. Jordan is full of him because he limns the low places with his presence, leaving traces of his glory everywhere. Finding him is a skill, yes, a discipline. But this pursuit results in intimate fellowship I can experience anywhere. I make a cup of tea at dawn and keep tryst with him while the doves on the power lines laugh at their inside jokes. I walk all the streets and talk to him while dodging cars and crossing impossible traffic. When I drive, he's in the car with me. He carries with me the burden of the stories I hear. Before I visit my friend in prison, I beg him to keep his promise—and then, on the other side of the glass, I see him dressed in a blue smock.

When I make mistakes in Arabic, he finds me in the pit of embarrassment. *I know humiliation,* he reminds me with a grin. When I sit on the fringes of fast conversations, feeling alien, he sits with me, that Word made flesh. And when I pick up toy cars and trains at the end of the day or make hummus sandwiches—again—I see him in the smiles of my sons curled up in the armchair together. I feel him in my husband's steady arms. No matter the challenges, I can wipe my tears and open my eyes to see hardy flowers rising in the sand.

As he gave Hagar buoying promises, so Christ promises me that exile is not the end of my story. I'm a sojourner on this arid earth, seeking a better country than Jordan or Palestine or the United States. By faith, I seek an unshakable kingdom, an everlasting one. I follow Christ's voice from the far side of a mirage—the quicksand of my own rebellion and the blinding injustices of the world.

Hajar, he calls me.

My spirit lifts. I am revived by his presence, crowned with the honor of being seen, known, and named. I am carried by the anticipation of glory.

PART 4

Revelation

CHAPTER 14

Field Guide to the New Jerusalem

I open my field guide to research poppies, and when I find them—**CROWN ANEMONE**, *Anemone coronaria*, parsley-like basal leaves—I read it's no longer illegal to pick them in the Holy Land, which surprises me, possessor of a journal filled with moldering, illegally picked Israeli wildflowers, but the field guide states that this now applies to all flora, that picking is encouraged because the factors that once promoted endangered species are no more, and the field guide continues by noting that red, color of anemones, is again a color of celebration, not of blood and of anger, a note that makes me turn the page, curious to read about **SQUIRTING CUCUMBERS**, *Ecballium elaterium*, with fruit green, bristly, and oblong, which explodes and squirts out seeds when ripe and exists purely to delight kids and their mothers who poke them with sticks, a comment that makes me jump, because I definitely have jabbed cucumbers with my boys, so I keep reading about **OLIVE TREES,** symbols of peace, not of resistance (since when had my field guide gotten snarky and political?) and about **THE TREE OF LIFE,** which produces different fruits each month and whose leaves are used for healing, and **WHEAT** that will satisfy all hunger and everyman's **VINE** and **FIG TREE,** and, curiouser and curiouser, I turn to Fauna where I find the **HOOPOE,** *Upupa epops,* a bird no longer considered unclean and no longer the national bird of the State of Israel (the State of Israel no longer existing, you see) and the **SUNBIRD,** *Cinnyris osea,* no longer the national bird of Palestine (since Palestine is finally free, even of itself), and I read of **NON-PREDATORY WOLVES** and the **LAMBS THAT LIE DOWN** with them, of **NON-POISONOUS COBRAS** and **LIVING CREATURES** full of eyes, and I turn to the book's cover, flummoxed, only to discover this isn't my old field guide, but a guide to someplace new, a place I've read about all my life and occasionally, with panic, doubted, but here is a guide to it with material verifying what I suspected to be true: a new creation has arrived, where dust storms and terrorism are not, where roads do not have checkpoints and walls are not built, where even light is not needed, because there's this **LAMB (see also LION)** and water is not scarce, because there is a **RIVER OF LIFE** quenching pilgrims who come unhindered to the praise of all nations, and I start to cry (out of joy) and then I remember, *Someone here will wipe my tears, someone I've longed for and loved,* so with my field guide in hand I step out to find him in the New Jerusalem.

CHAPTER 15

With This Stitch, I Hope

Palestinian history has been written in many forms
but the most beautiful and profound form
was written by the women of Palestine
from the north of Palestine to its south
with the needle that embroidered those dresses
that were colored by the sun.

—Nasser Soumi, Palestinian visual artist

Amman's old downtown, al-balad, is an assault on the five senses—in the best way possible. Shopkeepers advertise their wares with shouts, and vehicles of all sizes honk stridently. Over the heads of shoppers pushing strollers, lugging plastic bags of merchandise, and sipping fresh-squeezed juice, broadcast recordings repetitively praise Allah. Cigarette smoke and car exhaust mix with the scents of perfume, coffee, and boiled corn.

Portable wooden trays loaded with sweatpants and socks, belts and boxers, cram the sidewalks opposite stores selling strainers, drain covers, and light bulbs, souvenir sand bottles and painted pottery. You can buy mastic-flavored gum from children, or eat grilled shawarma slathered in garlicky mayonnaise, or taste melty cheese *kanafe* drenched in sugar-syrup off a Styrofoam plate. On more than one summer evening, I've come home from the balad to find my feet tattooed by grime between my sandal straps.

The balad's most eye-catching items for sale are thobes—hundreds of floor-length, heavily embroidered dresses arranged behind glass windows, parading outside of stores on headless mannequins or flapping in the wind from hangers in shop doorways. Most are black or white with machine stitching—cheaply manufactured—but some are hand-stitched or emblazoned with rhinestones, truly regal. Thobes make classic tourist gifts, but Jordanian women—around half of whom claim Palestinian ancestry—purchase them too and wear them for weddings, engagement parties, or national holidays.

Early in our time in Jordan, I heard that women living in historic Palestine had been able to identify one another's origins based on the embroidered designs—the *tatreez*—on their thobes. This concept intrigued me—an intertwining of place and craft, history and art—an idea completely lacking in this century's mass-produced fashion world.

As associate editor of an online publication, I assigned a Jordanian writer an article about thobes, hoping that somehow she would flesh out the notion that Arab women could once be identified by their dress. I wanted to know more. When Batool submitted the piece to me, she bubbled with excitement. "There's a whole museum about this!" she exclaimed. "You must go!"

What I recall from my first visit to the Tiraz Centre is a sense of enchantment as I wandered among antique thobes, shawls, jewelry, and accessories. Opened in central Amman in 2015, the museum houses Widad Kawar's collection of Arab dress. Comprised of more than 2,000 pieces, it's the largest existing collection of Palestinian and Jordanian dress in the world.

My second visit was a lightning mission to take a few photos for Batool's article—with my sons in tow. I flew around snagging pictures, while at one point my eight-year-old, David, was lying on his back on the floor with screaming, one-and-a-half year-old Adam clamped to his chest. After just a few minutes, I hauled the boys out the door, flashing an apologetic smile at the museum's curator. She looked flawless in a blouse and pressed slacks, with perfect hair and makeup. "I will come back another time, by myself," I told her.

"That will be better for me," she confessed.

Until my next visit, I contented myself with *Threads of Identity*, a heavy, glossy volume I splurged on in the name of research. Widad Kawar's book contained hundreds of full-page photographs, along with the stories of many of the women whose Palestinian thobes comprise her collection. Born in Tulkarem in the present-day West Bank in 1931, Kawar spent a portion of her childhood in Bethlehem. She recalls watching women from surrounding villages walk into the historically Christian town for Saturday morning market day wearing their embroidered thobes. These sights planted the seeds of her love for tatreez, an art Arab women in Palestine had been practicing and transmitting for generations.

In 1948, Kawar was a recent graduate of the American University of Beirut when Jewish military operations displaced around 700,000 Arabs from their ancestral lands to establish the state of Israel. The consequences for the Palestinian people were devastating; Palestinians call May 15th, the day Israel was founded, *al-Nakba*—the catastrophe. Kawar explains the far-reaching impact of Israel's modern birth on the Palestinian community:

> The wars and occupation of 1948 . . . destroyed hundreds of villages and dispossessed many of the Palestinian people, separating them from their extended families and driving them into exile. This caused a rupture in Palestinian society and culture, undermining familiar patterns of life. Particularly apparent was the disruption of rural life. Villagers, who were able to grow their own crops and make their own clothes, were reduced to dependence on rations and bare subsistence in refugee camps. Their colourful and richly embroidered handmade costumes were in danger of becoming extinct, for the refugee women lacked the means to continue making such dresses and were sometimes forced to sell the ones they had.

In 1967, when Israel assumed control of Gaza, the Golan Heights, and the West Bank, many Palestinians became refugees a second time. Thousands bled into Jordan, Lebanon, and Syria. Kawar remarks that Palestinian women "started selling on a grand scale," exchanging their thobes for money to sustain their families. Recognizing that the thobe was both an emerging symbol of Palestinian identity and a rapidly disappearing art form, Kawar, now settled in Amman with her husband, began purchasing the dresses. She always aimed to learn as much as she could about the women who'd sewn and worn them. "These women remain my chief inspiration," she writes in the introduction to *Threads of Identity*.

Now in her early 90s, Kawar's life has been one of research, publishing, international showings, and scholarly collaborations to preserve this art form. "The *thob* is a vivid symbol of the vibrant society and culture that prevailed in Palestine until the violent uprooting of its people," she says. "It attests to the Palestinians' determination to sustain their national identity and their hopes for the restoration of their rights."

* * *

In May 2021, my mind was consumed by the war between Israel and Hamas. Reacting in part to an Israeli court decision to evict Palestinians from their homes in East Jerusalem, Gaza-based Hamas launched hundreds of rockets into southern Israel, provoking a strong military response. At my in-laws' house in Arizona, far from my home in Amman, I sought a productive way to engage my physical body in the conflict, a helpful alternative to doom-scrolling. I registered for a Palestinian tatreez class.

Before the two-hour Zoom session on tatreez, I hoped I'd remember how to thread a needle. I'd learned to cross-stitch in high school as part of my rigorous home education. In addition to physics, Latin, and logic, my capable mother gave me a solid foundation in the kitchen and a familiarity with handcrafts. My cross-stitch project—a posse of wild animals surrounded by a geometric frame—frustrated me to no end. I miscounted holes in the Aida cloth and misplaced stitches, smashing my lion's face and crippling my lamb. On the back of my work, threads tangled, making it difficult to remove my mistakes.

Gratefully, I discovered that making stitches was like roller-skating after a long pause. Wafa Ghnaim, our tall Palestinian-American instructor who usually wore black, had founded Tatreez & Tea, an organization to preserve and revive the practice of Palestinian embroidery. She taught us to use thread economically, like Palestinian women in the early twentieth century. Keeping the backsides of our work clean was critical, she told us. Historically, embroidered dresses weren't museum pieces but garments that would be worn and could snag. "The less thread you use," she noted, "the lighter your end product."

As we stitched a chevron pattern originating from Gaza, she taught us about Majdal, a city in the Gaza area. Known as a weaving center in the early 1900s, weavers on 500 looms produced cloth for the region. When the State of Israel was established in 1948, Majdal's weaving industry was decimated. Most of the city's 10,000 residents fled under Israeli shelling, and the 2,500 who remained were confined to a barbed-wire ghetto and eventually trucked to Egypt.

Wafa told us that the Israeli city of Ashkelon stands where Majdal once existed, a fact that arrested me. During my two years living in Israel, I'd taken multiple trips to Ashkelon's beach but never once heard of the razed Palestinian city on which it had been built. I got curious—what else might be hidden about the land I had studied so thoroughly?

Between stitching tiny *x*s with scarlet thread, I talked and texted with Palestinian friends, compelled to broaden my understanding of their reality. "How do you feel?" I asked, as Israeli shells pounded the Gaza Strip in response to Hamas's rocket salvos. "Do you think there's a solution to the conflict? Why do Palestinians—even those who have never lived in Palestine—never forget their homeland?"

Ruba, a Jordanian-born Palestinian friend with relatives in the West Bank, patiently answered me over a period of days. In her recorded WhatsApp messages, her tone was soft but determined, like the one she'd used six years before when refusing to speak English with me so I'd learn Arabic. "Palestinian refugees—why don't they forget?" she replied. "Because you have an occupation, you have a side trying to erase your existence from your land. . . . In Palestine, the idea is that if one is quiet, if he doesn't keep protecting [his identity and heritage], if he doesn't defend it, there is a side that is trying to erase it slowly . . . trying to erase history."

Palestinians viewed tatreez as an act of resistance toward the Israeli occupation. To me it also seemed a kind of memorialization, a way to preserve a culture and understand a people in exile. I realized that delving into the Palestinian narrative would make a few in my circles uncomfortable, but I felt like tatreez was a safe way to dig into an often polarizing, volatile topic.

I picked up my needle, snipped an arm-length piece of thread, and began.

* * *

Pearl cotton embroidery thread comes spun on inch-long plastic tubes, eighty-seven yards wound in compact, neat balls. Seven colors—the colors for my Village Series project—arrived by mail at my parents' house in California, bedded in brown packaging. Even before finishing my chevrons, I'd signed up for the fourteen-week course. I was hooked.

Though some of the women in my class were customizing their projects by swapping colors, I felt nervous about experimenting. Besides, I liked the colors Wafa suggested in her design. Reds—my long-time favorite—were dominant. In her book *Tatreez & Tea,* Wafa notes that red traditionally signified lifeblood and happiness and was the most common color used for embroidery by Palestinian women of all ages prior to 1948.

When I first downloaded the Village Series pattern—a 12.5- by 16-inch design—I was stunned. Before me sat a Palestinian dress in miniature, an explosive mosaic of patterns, absolutely loaded with history. I balked. How was I, a mom of two and a former hater of cross-stitch, going to find the endurance to complete such a massive project?

As my classmates introduced themselves in our Signal chat, I was intimidated further. Some of the women—most of them Americans—called themselves textile artists. One of them shared that this was her "mindless project." Two were archaeologists, one specializing in Peruvian textiles. After listening to Wafa's opening lecture, they offered suggestions for stitching the first motif.

"I'd go down this row with method one, then go up and cross them."

"Here, I would use half-crosses, but full stitches around this corner. Like one, two, three, four."

I listened in wonder. My brain had no pathways to conceptualize their suggestions, so I sketched their ideas in my notebook, hoping I'd be able to follow my diagrams later. Apparently, my only advantage in this bunch was being an Arabic speaker with Palestinian friends—a leg-up that offered no help with the language of stitching.

When I turned to my Aida canvas, the piece of perforated cloth felt huge. Each vermillion stitch I added seemed like a pixel on a high-definition screen. Thankfully, though, I could relax during Wafa's history lectures. As she spoke about Jerusalem, Yaffa, and Bir as-Saba', Wafa shared public domain, black-and-white photographs. I recognized many of the places she highlighted from my years studying biblical geography. The locales were familiar. Yet in these images, ancient biblical sites and even some modern ones that I'd known as Israeli were populated by Palestinians. Arabs had lived in these places, embroidered in these places for hundreds of years before the Jewish people returned to the Holy Land en masse. Week after week, I saw geography reinterpreted, new layers of history laid down stitch by stitch.

Outside of class, I studied the origins of Arab embroidery. Hanan Munayer, a Haifa-born microbiologist and pharmaceutical researcher turned tatreez collector, unearthed evidence of ancient styles present in modern Palestinian designs. In a 2012 lecture at the Library of Congress, she talked about an ivory engraving depicting two Canaanite women wearing the unique fold-over dress still worn by Bedouin tribeswomen in the 1900s.

Tunics in the same cut as modern Palestinian thobes were found in Egyptian, Syrian, and Palestinian graves from the Roman era. The thobe's prominent square chest piece, called the *qabbeh* in Arabic, emerged from Spain's Andalucia region in the eleventh and twelfth centuries—the height of the Arab world's golden age.

Today, off-white linen with red cross-stitch is the color combination most often associated with Palestinian embroidery. Munayer highlighted ninth-century examples with the same colors found in Alexandria, Egypt. Everyday people had stitched with black and red thread on off-white tunics in thirteenth- through fifteenth-century Egypt, using geometric patterns that could have been pulled from twentieth-century thobes. On the Ashmolean Museum's website, I studied scraps of these tunics, zooming in as close as I could to observe the moldering linen. Rows and clumps of stitches surrounded by disintegrated fabric resembled lines of braille, caterpillar-consumed leaves.

* * *

The first time I heard the word qabbeh paired with the object it describes, I was standing at my dining room table with Manal. When she comes to clean our apartment, she often removes her headscarf, revealing her cropped, gray-streaked hair. It is always tied back, never free. Before filling the mop bucket, she might show me a bruise on her arm from her husband's hand, a burn caused by a flash of steam racing up her arm while cooking with a broken pot, a missing tooth. Sometimes she stands with her hands resting on her ample bosom, eyes drifting as she tells me about her son's latest challenges in elementary school or about her leaking toilet.

Though she knows her ancestors came from the region where Israelis built Ben Gurion International Airport, Manal doesn't flaunt her Palestinian identity. Perhaps that is because all her energy goes to sustaining her family. Besides cleaning foreigners' apartments, Manal cooks occasionally—big pots of *maqloubeh* with pieces of succulent fried eggplant and cauliflower. She also crochets hats and scarves and cross-stitches small pieces. Once, before my family traveled to the United States, I shopped for gifts from a plastic bag of her handwork. She laid her tatreez on the table: bookmarks, Christmas tree ornaments, wall hangings depicting camels.

"And this is a qabbeh," she said. She unfolded a piece of Aida cloth with frayed edges and spread it before me. The chest panel fairly pulsed—a rectangle emblazoned with dark red stitches, unfurling flowers with dabs of green, blue, and yellow at their centers, curvilinear designs edged by a row of dangling cypress trees.

"Wow, this is so pretty!" I exclaimed, wishing I knew more precise Arabic words to convey my meaning. I picked up the qabbeh, turned the cloth over in my hands. On the back, long, baggy threads crossed and jumped, obscuring the front's intricate, symmetrical pattern. Flipping the fabric again, my fingers traced the precise stitches.

After knowing Manal for years, I suddenly felt like I saw the kernel of her person. While her qabbeh's messy backside mirrored her public identity—she struggles with under-confidence and depression brought on by poverty, health problems, and abuse—the front revealed her potential in a thousand carefully placed stitches. I felt like Manal had been holding out on me, hiding behind her cute but insignificant bookmarks and ornaments. One hundred years ago, she would have created this piece for a thobe in her wedding trousseau, surrounded by female relatives swapping jokes and advice while they sewed up a storm. When she created this, had she sensed a cloud of women behind the shimmering scrim of time? Had she felt the sense of joyous expectation latent in her craft?

In the red flowers of a chest piece, I saw a creative woman who still had capacity for imagination and experimentation, though frequently limited by circumstance. When she stitched this, perhaps she had created out of more than a need for survival. Maybe while Manal embroidered, she had experienced calm, a sense of control and well-being, hope that her life could bloom like so many unfurling flowers.

* * *

Wafa taught us about Lifta, one of the most prosperous villages in the Jerusalem area before 1948. Like other nearby villages, its fashion was influenced by the styles of Bethlehem— chest panels thick with swirling *tahreeri* stitch, gold-colored *ghabbani* silk imported from Damascus and Aleppo. Lifta was known for its five olive presses that serviced the entire region. Residents farmed lands that stretched to the current walls of Jerusalem's Old City, a couple of miles to the southeast.

Lifta is a symbol of the Nakba. Erected during the Ottoman period, it is one of the only Arab villages not completely razed during the War for Independence. Homes feature elegantly arched windows nestled in twos and threes, ensconced beneath larger rainbow arches. On my first ride into Jerusalem, I glimpsed Lifta's ruins along Highway 1, embedded in the last undeveloped slope before west Jerusalem's burgeoning suburbs and cemeteries. On subsequent trips to Jerusalem, I recall how the pale limestone of Lifta's abandoned buildings contrasted with the vibrant grass.

Lifta currently functions as a recreational area for Israelis and Palestinians alike, a place they can picnic and swim in its spring-fed pool. But Jerusalem-born and Oxford-trained historian Walid Khalidi chronicles the village's darker history—its depopulation, along with that of more than 400 other Palestinian villages and hamlets.

In his seminal work, *All That Remains,* he writes that on December 28, 1947, five residents of Lifta were killed when members of the Stern Gang, a group of extremist Zionist freedom fighters, fired machine guns and threw grenades into a coffeehouse. As part of systematic attacks calculated to drive Arab residents from their homes, raids on Lifta and surrounding villages continued until February 1948, when Israel's future prime minister David Ben-Gurion declared that the entry to Jerusalem through Lifta was "one hundred percent Jews."

While I was beginning my Village Series project, the Israeli newspaper *Haaretz* ran an article on controversial plans to build villas on Lifta's ruins. The piece featured the story of Yehya Odeh and his family, who left the village in 1948. "The conditions were created that did not allow for life there anymore," Odeh said.

One day my father decided that we would leave the village. We all left, we ran into a truck with four other families from the village and joined them. The adults covered the children and we continued to Abu Ghosh. There we stopped because the day before they murdered a resident of Lifta there. So we traveled to Latrun, went up to Ramallah and there we remained refugees. We were in the clothes we left with and we didn't even have food. In an hour we went from kings in our village to refugees who are knocking on the doors of the wealthy to look for food.

As I viewed photographs of Lifta on *Palestine Remembered*, an online oral and visual history project, I saw peaceful beauty marred by intentional destruction. One picture showed rarified light pouring through blossoming almond trees; the next highlighted stone rooftops smashed in to prevent Arab homeowners from returning.

I always think of Lifta when leaving Amman through the northwestern neighborhood of Sweileh, on the route to al-Baqa'a, Jordan's largest Palestinian refugee camp. The highway there curves like Israel's Highway 1 on the approach to Jerusalem. Sunlight strikes the eucalyptus trees and exposed bedrock in a way that makes my brain react involuntarily, pumping adrenaline down pathways chiseled by so many anticipation-spiked climbs to the holy city. I reflexively look out the car window, searching for Lifta.

But Lifta is not there. A corridor of nurseries flashes by, followed by gas stations, coffee shops, an Orthodox church. Then I remember: I'm in Jordan, a place of Palestinian exile.

* * *

One jet-lagged night after returning from Arizona and California, I stood near the windows of our sunroom in Amman reading poems by streetlight. In the haze of sleep deprivation, in that place where my soul had not yet caught up with my body, the poems drew me from America back to Jordan. Their poignant imagery pierced my blurry mind—talk of gilded limestone buildings and iridescent, chorusing sunbirds, the dawn call to prayer followed by coffee and Fairouz's dreamy singing voice.

Outside the window in daylight, another image pierced my consciousness: a blue Star of David spray-painted in the middle of the street. In the coming days, we saw detritus of the Gaza war all over the city: slogans graffitied on walls—*Palestine must be free, from the river to the sea*—billboards and banners stating the distance from Amman to the al-Aqsa mosque in Jerusalem, six-pointed stars and Israeli flags painted on trash dumpsters. The star on the street hit me the hardest, though, perhaps because it jerked me out of the pleasantly curated teaching I'd been receiving about Palestinians on Zoom. Suddenly I remembered that Palestinians weren't perfect—embroidery and poetry aside.

Across the street lived my neighbor, a mother of five whose father hailed from Ludd in western Palestine. In May I had texted her from Arizona about the conflict.

The land and the nation cannot be divided, and Palestine will return, she messaged me. *The Jews will leave it—and it doesn't matter to us where they go. God willing, they'll all die and there will be no trace of them left.*

The bitterness in her tone had knocked the wind out of me. When I gently asked how she could live with such a powerful emotion inside (I suggested hatred), she said it wasn't hatred. I offered that perhaps violence wasn't the answer, mentioned the possibility of forgiveness, reconciliation.

Really? she replied. *You want to love those who stole your land and destroyed your homes and killed your children?*

Now I stared out the window toward my neighbor's building and wondered if I'd ruined our friendship. My suggestions had probably smelled of normalization to her, *tatbee'a* in Arabic, a word I'd learned by watching a satirical Jordanian news show on YouTube. Though normalization broadly refers to Arab nations establishing political relations with Israel, I saw practical, daily life examples around me too. Once an Egyptian actor posted a picture on social media of himself with an Israeli friend. Hurricanes of condemnation slammed the actor from around the Arab world. "How can you be friends with the occupation? You're opening the door to normalization." This anti-normalization sentiment was wildly popular, and those who dissented were shamed or silenced by the majority.

I remember feeling profoundly uncomfortable with this idea. How could we ever hope for peace in the Middle East if Arabs and Jews couldn't even post a picture together without accusations of compromise? I struggled to communicate this idea to my Arabic teacher, but my political opinions in English lack power, much less in my second language.

In the language of tatreez at least, I was growing in fluency. I stitched in the margins of my day, during Adam's nap time and after the boys went to bed. More than one needle rusted between my sweaty fingers. I began a row of eight-pointed stars, marveling at how they resembled poinsettias. When I discovered that I'd misplaced my initial motif, I picked out the bold petals, leaving behind red fuzz in the enlarged squares. The thread came out kinked as I loosened each stitch. Tearing out sounded muffled, like the ripping of cotton fabric.

* * *

How do we take a village like Lifta and repopulate it? Reconstruct a lifestyle from tatters?

As I embroidered, I wanted more than colorful *x*s to shape my imaginings about village life in Palestine. In the small but well-stocked library in our neighborhood in Amman, serendipity led me to *Portrait of a Palestinian Village*. The book contains more than 200 photographs taken by Hilma Granqvist, a Finnish anthropologist who spent three years in Artas, a village southwest of Bethlehem, between 1925 and 1931. She planned to research and write a book about women in Bible times.

On the book's title page, Granqvist wears leather Mary Janes and thick stockings, a plaid dress that falls beneath her knees. She looks directly at the camera—round, pale cheeks lifted in a smile and eyes squinted—as she models a traditional village cap. Silver chains beneath her chin fasten a dark shawl. A village woman stands on her left, reaching across Granqvist to adjust its fringe.

Granqvist's initial plan to write about biblical women was derailed—for in Artas, a village of 500, she discovered a vibrant, distinct, and living culture. Her research narrowed in on significant life events in a typical Palestinian village: pregnancy, birth, circumcision, engagement, marriage, and death. According to her field notes, Artas's residents lived in one-room limestone houses with courtyards where they completed much of their work. Lives rotated around agriculture and raising animals. Once a week, they sold their produce in Bethlehem, a two-and-a-half-mile walk away.

Flipping through *Portrait*, I pause at a picture of a woman carrying her one-year-old son on her shoulder. I wonder what attracts me to her in particular. I like how she is barefoot in her packed dirt courtyard, backed by the stone wall of her house and a sleek cow. (I would be barefoot too, a habit my Jordanian neighbor scolds me for.) I like how her son, in contrast, wears smart little boots and a coat. He has a full head of hair, as Arab kids tend to, one hand in his chubby mouth, the other draped casually over his mother's white-shawled head. Her dress is nothing to speak of. In fact, the pieces, seamed with *manajel* stitch, look like they were dyed in different vats. She draws her eyebrows together against the sun and wears a smirk—an expression conveying confidence and competence.

This woman was one of the *fellahin*—Arabic for farmers living in villages. I found myself considering this word closely when reading the *Palestine Royal Commission Report* from 1937, an original, blue-backed gem I found in a Jordanian bookstore. The report, compiled by the British Mandate government in the midst of an Arab revolt against their administration in Palestine, describes the fellahin as "backward peasantry."

Gratefully, backward is no longer a word we use to describe people; condescending superiority toward outsiders is no longer in vogue. But what did the British intend when employing this word? Why does their posture toward the fellahin contrast so sharply with the respect conveyed through Granqvist's research and photographs?

The fellahin's lifestyle was simple, barely touched by the Industrial Revolution. Poverty was a reality, access to public services lean. While such a life is nothing to be coveted or glorified, I wonder if the report's use of "backward" intends to contrast the indigenous Arabs with the generally young, educated Jewish people of European descent who were flooding into Palestine under Mandate-sponsored immigration plans. Did calling the fellahin backward help minimize their status as landowners? Did it bolster the popular saying that Palestine was "a land without a people for a people without a land"? (Statistics show that in 1936, close to a million Arabs lived in the Holy Land.)

The report's focus on the fellahin ignores the inhabitants of Arab cities—Jerusalem, Bethlehem, Ramallah, Jaffa, Haifa, Gaza, and Nablus—with their schools, cafés, printing presses, government organizations, religious institutions, and tourism companies. Thomas Reid, one of the partition commission's advisors, seemed to decry this emphasis on the peasants. "We are not dealing here with primitive people," Reid states in his objections to the partition plan laid out in 1938, "but with Arabs who can think politically and would almost certainly resist discriminating and indefensible treatment, even in the detested parcellation of their native land."

When I think of the peasant women embroidering in villages like Artas, I find proof that they were neither backward nor uncivilized. I imagine the strength and coordination required to bring water from the spring every morning, to grind wheat, bake bread before sunrise, wash laundry by hand, grow all my family's food, collect firewood, keep my home clean, and care for my children.

And somehow, I would still find time to stitch in a sunny corner of my courtyard, the knobby limestone wall against my back. My older son would herd chickens to the coop. My toddler would tumble into my lap, pulling my thread taut. I would whip stitches into cloth, needle blinking in the sun, the smell of manure rising around me.

* * *

As we prepared to move to a new part of Amman, to be closer to Austin's work and David's school, I decided to record the names of our current neighborhood's streets. From the time we moved there in 2015, I'd been told that Jabal al-Hussein was first settled by Palestinian refugees—that's why most of the streets were named after historic villages and cities. I loaded Adam in the stroller, grabbed my notebook and pencil, and started walking.

I couldn't even get off our street without recording a name—Bab al-Wad, an area in the valley leading from Tel Aviv to Jerusalem, very close to the place we'd lived in Israel. To the west, the street parallel to ours was Qalqiliya. To the east were Silwan, Kafr Bir'im, and Kafr Qasem. Farther away were 'Akka and Lod, al-Nasra and Majdal, Gaza, Safad, al-Karmal, Bir as-Saba'.

All over the neighborhood, I paused to write. Dust coated my sandaled feet and matted the hem of my skirt. Adam sat patiently in the shade of the stroller's umbrella, a cracker in hand. I recorded city names in Arabic letters beneath my embroidery class notes, then jammed the pencil into my messy bun and kept walking.

Sometime after my walk, I went to the library to read about some of these villages in *All That Remains*, published in 1992. I settled at a table with the tome, complied by a team of researchers from Birzeit University in Ramallah, the Institute for Palestine Studies in Washington, D.C., and the Galilee Center for Social Research. *All That Remains* gathers the research, photographs, and statistics that resulted from their four years studying "lost" villages in Palestine.

In his introduction, editor Khalidi says the book is not an attempt to delegitimize Zionism or rewrite history but rather "a call . . . for a pause, for a moment of introspection." He explains that although major cities from historic Palestine still exist, the villages and hamlets suffered a different fate:

> By the end of the war [1949], hundreds of entire villages had not only been depopulated but obliterated, their houses blown up or bulldozed. While many of the sites are difficult to access, to this day the observant traveler of Israeli roads and highways can see traces of their presence that would escape the observation of a casual passerby: a fenced-in area—often surmounting a gentle hill— of olive and other fruit trees left untended, of cactus hedges and domesticated plants run wild. Now and then a few crumbled houses are left standing, a neglected mosque or church, collapsing walls along the ghost of a village lane, but in the vast majority of cases all that remains is a scattering of stones and rubble across a forgotten landscape.

I paged through the Jerusalem section, encountering so many familiar places, villages between Jerusalem and the Israeli moshav where Austin and I had lived. Looking at the black-and-white photo of al-Qastel's ruined fortress, I could almost smell the spring grass and feel the sun pressing warmth into my skin. How many times did I go to the Mevasseret Mall and not dash across the highway to visit Kastel, the Hebraicized name for al-Qastel? At the entry for 'Ayn Karem, I remembered strolling its lanes while celebrating our second anniversary. Why had I only known that village as John the Baptist's birthplace? Why did no one tell me that the swanky restaurant we dined in was likely a converted Arab house?

For years, I had known that my education in the Holy Land favored the Israeli narrative. I realized that history had been told selectively, albeit without malicious intent. For some reason, though, as I sat in the library in Amman, the knowledge that I'd been taught only half of the story overwhelmed me viscerally. I paused my reading, took a deep breath. Nausea lifted my stomach. I felt destabilized, like the beginnings of an earthquake were trembling outward from my core.

In Caesarea as a college student, I marveled at Herod the Great's ancient building projects and the blue Mediterranean Sea. Had my professors not pointed out the minaret of Qisarya's mosque, a city where 960 Palestinians lived before Israel's War of Independence? Had biblical history engulfed the modern, melding Palestinian ruins with Herodian ones? In Shoresh, an Old Testament site visited by Samson, I posed with other cheerful nineteen- and twenty-year-olds in the forest. Something in me shakes as I read that a village called

Saris stood in the same location. Israelis plowed it under and planted a forest on top of it.

In the library I realized, maybe for the first time, how close I had lived to Deir Yassin, an Arab village of 750 where around 100 had been killed by Jewish paramilitary groups. Four, five miles maybe? I felt light-headed, disoriented. How was it I visited all these biblical and Israeli sites but never paused at the location of the infamous massacre, the event that had ignited fear of similar killings in villages all over Palestine? Had my younger self not cared about Palestinians?

Momentarily, I felt split in two, unrecognizable. Younger me wearing a baggy blue T-shirt emblazoned with a Star of David while posing on an Israeli tank stared at current me, Arabic-speaking tatreezer embedded among the largest population of Palestinians in exile. The two Heathers eyed one another suspiciously, despised one another.

Ilham, the assistant librarian (Palestinian—who would have guessed?) photocopied for me several pages from *All That Remains*. I left with a sheaf of papers and a brooding heart. How would I reconcile the two stories I'd been told? Was it possible to hold the Jewish narrative in one hand and the Palestinian in the other and hold on for the ride? I was aware of no models around me, no example to follow. Just recalcitrant Palestinians who call their fallen terrorists martyrs. Palestinians who seem unable to compromise. Palestinians who, in their art and storytelling, are stuck in 1948. Palestinians who seem to have stunted imaginations for the future.

But even as I felt acutely aware of their foibles and faults, I loved them. I loved their generosity, their steadfastness and resilience, their persistent calls for justice. I wanted people to hear their narrative, even though it didn't always satisfy, even though I outright rejected parts of it. I wanted all the millions of tourists in the Holy Land to see both religious history and modern history, Israelis and Palestinians, to embrace the ambiguous flood.

Was it possible, I wondered, in our telling of history, to celebrate a country reborn without erasing a culture ruptured? To acknowledge the victories gained by one side while mourning the injustices incurred by the other? Was it possible to tell a story that does not value one people more than another? To tell a full version of history—raucous, dissonant, and gray—and still look to the future with hope?

* * *

In our new apartment, snips of thread joined pulverized Cheerios on the carpet. They gathered in corners with dust from the nearby road under construction. I stitched the twirling candy-cane stripes of Jericho; rhythmic, wave-like snails from Galilee; a fringe border that felt like laying train track. Gaza's filigreed cypress trees, like knit lace, required concentration. A solid band from a Hebron-area thobe made my thumb joints ache from gripping cloth and needle. Wafa taught us about the two intifadas—*uprisings*—against Israel, helped us imagine living under restrictive curfews with the fear of indiscriminate arrest. I wondered if the women stitched to soothe their skittish nerves.

Tatreez turned out to be a conversation starter with my new neighbors. Um Omar said she doesn't have patience for stitching, but she eagerly shared stories about her grandparents. Her great-grandfather was a village leader under the British Mandate. During the Nakba, one of her relatives saw a baby in its mother's arms shot in the head while their family retreated under Jewish military fire.

Her grandfather was arrested by the Israeli police at age fifteen. While working in prison ironing uniforms, he and fellow inmates squirreled away enough gas to blow a hole in the prison wall and escape. He was shot in the legs while fleeing but still made it to Jordan on foot.

Less than a year before I met her, Um Omar's mother died. "Her sisters—my aunts—live in Gaza," she told me. "The Israelis didn't give them permits to come to the funeral."

Stories layered on stories. Hafsa—with warm, powdery cocoa skin and a sonorous voice—was an embroidery hobbyist like me. Though she moved to Amman when she got married, she is blessed among Palestinians, for she grew up in the Holy Land. She was born in Jerusalem, where her ancestors moved for trade and so they could easily pray in al-Aqsa, the mosque near the iconic Dome of the Rock. Though she was born there, she does not have a Jerusalem ID card and needs a special permit from Israeli authorities to enter the city. Her grandfather worked as a guard and translator for tourists in the Nativity Church in Bethlehem, but his family lived in a village nearby.

"What was the name of the village?" I asked.

"Artas."

My eyes bugged. "Are you serious?" Granqvist's photographs flooded back to me. Hafsa informed me that the Arabs of Artas were not expelled in 1948, though the city currently sits in Israel-proper. Her family still owns land there, a piece on a hill, not really suitable for a house. Under current Israeli laws, the state could confiscate their land at any time because it's unoccupied.

In addition to sharing her family's history, Hafsa explained the concept of *al-'awda*—return—and its centrality in Palestinian thought. In Palestinian refugee camps, elderly people still possess the keys of their former homes. They can't fathom abandoning their houses or land or country.

"They're holding on to the hope of return," she elaborated. "They say, 'One day, certainly, we will return. Of course we will take back our land. Of course our land will be liberated.'"

* * *

Our move didn't slow my visits to Tiraz. A good friend joked that I needed to buy a season pass. On my birthday, I brought a group of American and British friends to the museum to see the thobes.

"You can touch them if you want," our guide told us after explaining an exhibit.

"Really?" we gasped collectively.

"Yes, it's part of the experience," she replied glibly.

Within moments, I was on my knees, lifting hems to examine the backside of the stitching. I discovered bands of fabric reinforcing hemlines and sections of hems that had become tattered. I felt the supple coolness of handwoven linen, handled the magnificence of a Ramallah headscarf from the 1880s—straw-colored linen covered in swans, roosters, harps, feathers, and palms in red and black.

Wafa had remarked more than once in embroidery class, "If you're ever in the presence of a thobe . . ." I jotted down the whimsical phrase, smiled at how it evoked meeting a celebrity.

But her sentiments were true, one hundred percent. I experience that feeling when entering the quiet of Tiraz. The garments around me bear witness. They whisper testimonies. Surrounded by patterns I spent hours stitching, I feel engulfed by a crowd of friends, loved ones placing warm hands on my shoulders.

Here is a thobe from the Bethlehem region—fabric in bold magenta, red, and orange stripes, chest panel replete with gold tahreeri stitch. The dress hangs on a horizontal pole, sleeves smoothed into an exuberant gesture of welcome. When I notice sweat stains on the underarms, the dress's wearer springs to mind, dancing hard at weddings.

This dress has loose stitches on an underarm, stains on the shoulders, perhaps from a child's sticky hands. (I know how often my toddler plasters me with hummus.) Nearby I see a qabbeh attached to its thobe with red running stitch. *Was it carried over from another dress?* I wonder. Also, its owner did her mending in red—did she not care what people thought, or did she not have time to find a darker color?

On my way out one day, I asked the curator who'd once been startled by my rambunctious sons if I could possibly meet Widad Kawar. Several months later, the ninety-three-year-old received me warmly in her home. She wore a red-and-black argyle sweater and walked with a cane. Her stature is tiny, her smile bright. In a disarming manner, she told me she's glad I'm researching tatreez, the topic to which she's dedicated her life.

I didn't really want to hear about tatreez that day though. As someone whose life spanned the timeline of significant events in Palestinian history, I wanted to hear her thoughts on the future for Palestinians.

"I hope there will be some kind of peace," Kawar told me, "any kind of peace where people can go back to their villages and their homes, even though it will be so complicated and difficult because much of the land has been built on. But there must be some kind of settlement. They cannot stay for life as refugees—they must settle in some way or another that pleases both sides, that will please Israel and will please the Arabs."

Kawar expressed how the economic situation, especially for Palestinians living in refugee camps in Lebanon, Syria, Jordan, and Palestine, continues to decline year by year. Survival becomes more and more difficult. Young people in desperate situations easily turn to demonstrations and violence. She suggested that trade schools—few and far between in Jordan, at least—be established to train young men in basic jobs like cooking, carpentry, and gardening.

"What do you think about normalization?" I asked. Most young Palestinians I knew opposed normalizing political and relational ties with Israel. I was curious what someone of her age and experience would say.

"Everything stops with [the anti-normalization effort,]" Kawar responded. "It doesn't move. We want something to move. We want to get back to normal life."

* * *

By the time I visited al-Baqa'a, I had framed my Village Series sampler and hung it above our couch. I went to the Palestinian refugee camp about twelve miles north of Amman to meet women employed by a company that produces customized thobes. These ladies embroidered entire dresses—chest panels, sleeves, sweeping branches from waist to hem. Together they could produce a dress in less than two months.

"Besides the financial benefit, we practice our country's culture in this way," Um Ahmad told me. "We preserve our identity. This is our culture and our heritage."

When Um Ahmad sent me the pin to the camp, I opened Google maps to see streets packed, grid-like, in a tiny area. This was a distinguishing factor of the camps, I realized. Because residents initially lived in tents that were eventually replaced by prefabricated buildings, today's cement block structures cram the space. Only small alleys and lanes cut between shoddy structures.

In al-Baqa'a—Jordan's largest camp, home to more than 100,000—I tentatively parked as close to a wall as possible before slipping out of the car. Um Ahmad met me in the street wearing a plain black abaya, her sturdy face framed by a tan headscarf. We shook hands, and she led me to a building across from a mosque.

Inside, I sat with several women and piles of their embroidery. I cooed and marveled over their work, much of it done on white crepe fabric with stiff, perforated waste canvas basted on top. They described how, after finishing the cross-stitch, they'd snip around this plain marking fabric and extract the threads with fingernails and tweezers, leaving the perfectly placed tatreez behind.

Even before this explanation, though, I was introduced to Um Salah. A tiny, elderly woman, she sat beside me on the couch wearing a nightgown with butterflies on it. A white, lace-edged hijab circled her wrinkled face. I recalled an Arabic teacher once telling me, "Oh, Heather, if you ever get the chance to talk to an old person who lived through the Nakba, you must." I was ready to listen.

Um Salah was born in the late 1930s in 'Ajjur, a town northwest of Hebron. 'Ajjur's residents had heard about the Deir Yassin massacre, so when Jewish forces reached their town, they fled under fire, unarmed and afraid. They walked from village to village, sometimes sleeping on the plowed ground between trees, before reaching Jericho, where they lived in a tent in weather Um Salah described as fire. Eventually, they continued to the Dheisheh camp in the Bethlehem area.

"We stayed day after day, month after month, and year after year," she said. "We stayed a long time, and we grew up, and we became old women."

Dheisheh Camp, one of nineteen UNRWA-administered camps in the West Bank, still houses around 15,000 people. There are twelve official camps in Lebanon, nine in Syria, eight in the Gaza Strip, and ten in Jordan. In these camps, after the Nakba and again after the Six-Day War, displaced women from all over Palestine picked up their needles with new determination. Torn away from their stable village lifestyle and suddenly mixed with women from other areas, regional embroidery styles swirled. Thobes adorned with Palestine's green, red, black, and white flag appeared, and dresses bearing Jerusalem's iconic Dome of the Rock and calligraphed words like *Jerusalem* and *Palestine*. Instead of embroidering for themselves, women began to stitch for survival, selling their handwork through charities and businesses. Even Um Salah, an octogenarian, still embroiders for pay.

"What do you hope for your people in the future?" I asked the women. "What are your dreams for Palestinians?"

Um Ahmad replied simply. "We hope that we will all return to our land, that all Palestinians will be gathered in Palestine."

While the majority of Palestinians in Jordan enjoy the full rights of Jordanian citizenship, as a whole, Palestinians regularly refer to their "right of return." Al-'awda, in Arabic, is codified in UN Resolution 194 from December 1948. For everyday people, though, al-'awda is not just legalese. Palestinians consider the right of return a basic building block in any sustainable peace agreement between Israel and the Palestinian people.

Our conversation then turned intensely political. I had to draw on all my reserves of Arabic and my knowledge of history and current events to keep up. The women talked over one another, frenzied. One of them chain-smoked as they listed grievances, fomenting a churning whirlpool.

"The killing of the journalist Shireen Abu Akleh . . ."

". . . it was on purpose . . ."

"Can you imagine? They shot at them while they were worshipping!"

"They were just trying to pray."

"They're really suffering in Gaza . . ."

". . . no electricity, no water . . ."

"And then they arrest children, and demolish houses . . ."

"And they build settlements—how are we going to return if they keep stealing our land?"

Inside, I knew the Israeli counterarguments to their accusations, the terminology Jewish and many Western media outlets would use to describe these events. *The demolished homes were built without permits. Terror groups offer cash to families whose children are arrested or killed for the cause. Worshipers on the Temple Mount were throwing rocks at security forces.* But for now I just listened and absorbed their pain.

Hugging a couch pillow to her belly, Um Ahmad began to weep.

* * *

One of the last motifs I embroidered on my Village Series sampler is reminiscent of cyclamen. These flowering plants seem partial to growing out of porous limestone, often hiding in the crags of crumbling rock walls. Many times, I stumbled upon them in Israel, and I do here in Jordan too. I bend over a rock to find upside-down pink flowers lifted by reddish stems. Life flourishing in unlikely places, hope springing from unexpected ground.

How I long to practice the discipline of hope—a quality that resembles faith, that intentionally diverts thoughts of despair and imagines the fulfillment of dreams. I want to believe in a hope and a future for Palestinians in diaspora: for exiles in Jordan, many of whom have Jordanian passports but still cannot travel to where their grandparents were born; in Lebanon, where after seventy-five years they're still stateless refugees; in Syria, where some are doubly displaced by civil war; in the West Bank and Gaza, where they face movement restrictions, degrading treatment at checkpoints, punitive raids and home demolitions, administrative detention in Israeli prisons. All people who want to find home.

By the time I hung my sampler on the living room wall—nearly 20,000 stitches made over five months of effort—the act of stitching had become imbued with meaning. Tatreez had become a tangible expression of hope. I find stitching a creative act of resistance—*muqawama* in Arabic—providing me with space to combat denial and erasure of Palestinian history and heritage. Tatreez allows me to symbolically express my longings for my Palestinian friends and neighbors.

May they experience stability and settledness. May they be freed from bitterness and the need for revenge. May they be healed from compounding traumas. May they find a future that does not compromise the security or self-determination of others. May they resist cultural norms to achieve a just peace. May they be well.

With the most basic materials—needle, cloth, and thread—I can reject despair, violence, and death. Every stitch becomes a vision of future peace, equal opportunity, and bright prospects. Every stitch a hope, a dream, a wordless prayer.

CHAPTER 16

These Common Threads

A fictional story based on true events

"It was crowded in the transit camp, so crowded."
That's the first thing Saeda told her granddaughter
Lior and her friends when they tumbled into her flat
after picnicking near the ruins of Rosh HaAyin. As part of their
army service, two of them were dabbling in Arabic (the blonde-
haired, blue-eyed one—Ashkenazi for sure—and the one who
wore glasses and still had acne). They wanted to know what it
had been like, being Jewish in Yemen. Lior told them, "Let's go
see my grandma and you can ask her." So they came, with sun-
kissed shoulders and cut-off shorts.

Saeda liked it when they came around. They invaded the
kitchen to make coffee, boisterous and chatty, and Lior came
to her armchair to kiss her cheek—tousled hair, olive skin, a
silver Magen David twinkling on her chest. She smelled like
the eucalyptus trees near the crumbling Turkish fort, like the
brackish water of the pond.

"Could you show them your embroidery too?" Lior asked, so close her curls tickled Saeda's nose. So Saeda shuffled to the bureau in her room and brought out the cuffs of the *sirwal* she'd worn on the plane from Aden to Tel Aviv.

The transit camp had been crowded, she told the girls, once they settled down with their coffees and cigarettes. Fifty-thousand Yemenite Jews like her filtering in from Aden and Sana'a and the mountain villages. For months she and Yehya and the girls—Lior's mama and her aunt—lived in a lopsided tent in a mass of other lopsided tents, gathered like Ezekiel's dry bones. *I know the plans I have for you,* the LORD promised, *plans to prosper and not to harm you.*

They waited their turn. Saeda told them about the day a group of foreigners came to their section of the camp with a scale. Rumors flickered from tent to tent. "We can't bring everything; we'll have to leave anything heavy." Saeda flashed a glance at Yehya as he grabbed the kettle, a cooking pot, and a roll of bedding, then strode out to be weighed. He didn't ask what she thought they should bring to *Eretz Yisrael*.

"And I said to myself," Saeda recalled, "aren't they calling this a magic carpet?" A magic carpet would carry all of it—the candlesticks she lit every Friday evening, the heavy pot she packed with dense, oily *jachnoon* to bake overnight for Shabbat morning. On those Saturdays, Yehya would go to the synagogue for prayers, melodic Hebrew hallelujahs rising from the building half-sunk into the ground so it wouldn't stand higher than the Muslim-owned buildings around it. Eventually, here in Israel, European Jews told Yehya that their dialect was the most beautiful, most accurate Hebrew still living, what with Arabic and Hebrew being

semitic cousins, the roots of so many words intertwined, indistin-
guishable. *Shemesh, shams,* sun. *Beit, bayt,* house.

The plane will be crowded, Saeda had thought, *so crowded,
we can't bring everything.* Her mind scuttled over the contents of
the tent—her silver jewelry Yehya had designed himself, with its
intricate, hammered filigree. The strips of embroidery she had
stitched in the camp to sew on the girls' clothes in the future, in
their new home. She needed to keep her hands busy while they
waited, while she tried not to think about the eighty-two Jews
murdered in Aden, about the looting and destruction of their
businesses when their Muslim neighbors attacked them after
Palestine's partition.

Yehya bowed back into the tent. "What'd they say?" Saeda
asked.

"There's not enough room. We can buy new things when
we arrive."

"But I can't leave the candlesticks," Saeda whispered,
panicked, frantic. She felt her heart beating like a bird's.

"You have to."

"I can wear my jewelry, and we'll put the embroidery in your
pockets."

"It's still weight, Saeda."

They stared at each other until Saeda whipped herself away.
No, no, no. Going to the Promised Land shouldn't be like this.
Every year at Pesach they said, "Next year in Jerusalem," and
she meant it, right? Her whole life she'd prayed toward that city,
imagining it in a hazy kind of way, a way that felt like looking
into a distant dream. Jerusalem, a place of milk and honey, of
light and the Messiah.

She should be grateful now. Glad. *My heart rejoices in the God of my salvation.* The girls would grow up in Eretz Yisrael, safe from discrimination, safe from laws that could forcibly convert them to Islam.

"They say to leave anything non-essential," Yehya told her. But these objects that grounded her identity, weren't they essential? The candlesticks, two flames that had anchored every week of her life in rhythms of rest, over which she'd prayed the *bracha* her mother taught her from so young. The necklace Yehya had fastened around her neck at their wedding, when already she'd been weighed down by flowers and palm fronds, her hands hennaed, the hem of her dress left undone in memory of the fallen Temple. The careful rows of fly and chain stitch, the medallions and webs that identified her in Yemen's community, the skill that set her apart from Muslim women, whose husbands came to Yehya with their wives' orders for edging their garments.

"As-salaamu aleikum," they had greeted Yehya.

She didn't speak their version of Arabic, but she knew that greeting. *Salaam. Shalom.* Peace. They had spoken those words even as they perpetuated laws that boxed Jews into specific occupations—silversmithing, carpentry, weaving, things like that. Even as they forced Yehya to remove his shoes when he entered their marketplaces and banned him from wearing a dagger at his waist like all Yemeni men.

Saeda stared down at the cuffs spread on her knees, glimmering with silver and gold threads tacked down in swirls. She had worn these when they shuffled down the airstrip in Yemen, surrounded by jagged mountains. She had craned her neck to stare at smiling men in smart caps and uniforms, women with uncovered hair wearing crisp collared shirts. They assisted the crowd up the movable staircase and into the enormous, idling jet, its fuselage emblazoned with an American flag. Saeda heard they'd ripped out the normal seating and replaced it with wooden benches so they could fit more people inside. She retreated beneath her *gargush*, fastened closely under her chin. Its beaded fringe wavered in the wind.

She shuddered as she and Yehya stepped forward, gripping the girls' hands. Even in their isolation at the end of the Arabian Peninsula, they had heard of the awful things that happened to their fellow Jews in Europe during the war—millions rounded up and herded onto railcars, women and kids separated from the men. They'd been stripped of their clothes, their glasses and shoes piled up, their heads shaved. Smokestacks had pumped out wraithlike towers of smoke. *Shoah*, they called it—an ancient word given new meaning. *Catastrophe.*

But now, today, leaving is a choice, Saeda reminded herself on the airstrip. *We are going to Yerushalayim. Baruch HaShem. Blessed are you, LORD our God, King of the universe.*

She glanced at Yehya for reassurance. His earlocks lifted in the hot, artificial wind from the roaring jet engines. At the front of the line, she saw an old man being relieved of a bed roll, a woman coaxed to leave an extra bundle behind. She thought of herself crouching in the corner of their tent, tossing her necklace onto a pile. She remembered the candlesticks clattering, how the strips of stitching had rolled from her palms like ribbons.

Lior and her friends had knelt around Saeda and examined her stitching. When they arrived in Israel, she told them, they were transferred to an encampment in Rosh HaAyin, a marshy area inland from the Mediterranean. ("There's some more words for you—*Rosh HaAyin, Ras al-'Ayn* in Arabic—don't you hear the similarity?") They were received jubilantly by other newly minted Israelis—the Yemenite Jews had survived, the whole lot of them!—but life had felt explosive in those early years, teeming with dissonance and altered expectations. In Yemen, her life had been carefully delineated. In Israel, societal norms were dashed, all these Jews mixing together, the ones from Europe finding the Yemenites so exotic and yet provincial at the same time.

She told the girls how she'd been hired at a handcrafts workshop, how strange it had been working under Ashkenazi and Sephardic supervisors. They changed the embroidery patterns the Mizrahi women had stitched since girlhood, using symmetry and colors that would appeal to tourists. She worked long hours so the girls could go to school. Yehya found employment as a farmer, something he wasn't used to at all.

One of Lior's friends mentioned an embroidered blouse her mom had in her closet. Another said she'd heard Arab women had an affinity for stitching too. The conversation accordioned outward, and Saeda sat on the fringe, waiting for them to listen again. She recalled an afternoon in Jerusalem when she saw an Arab woman her age wearing a black dress with hand-stitched flowers. Saeda's heart had practically jumped out at her.

Now, she sat alone in her dusky room. The sun descended toward the Mediterranean, light coming through the dusty geraniums on the windowsill. The girls had washed up before they left—she smelled the citrusy pop of dish soap over subtle notes of cardamom and smoke. Maybe she had tired them with her stories. Maybe she had said too much.

But there was so much more she wanted to say. She wanted to tell them how in the Old City, when poking around in souvenir shops, she had always greeted shopkeepers in Arabic, just to watch their faces spark with surprise. They left before she could tell them that when she watched the evening news, she could catch a few words of the Palestinian Arabic before the Hebrew dubbing came on—tension in the West Bank, IDF raids in Jenin, a mother weeping for her imprisoned child.

She wished she could sit with some of those Arabs sometime and just listen to their stories, maybe tell some of hers. She fingered the stitched medallion on her left knee. She wished she could bring her embroidery along and hold it before them like flags of peace.

CHAPTER 17

Braiding Challah

More than a year before October 7, 2023—the day Israelis call Black Sabbath—I made challah in Jordan for the first time. While Adam chattered about M&M's and airplanes and driving a fast car, I poured warm water in a mixing bowl. A comforting smell arose: yeast awakening.

Dough clung raggedly to my hand while I kneaded. On Friday afternoons in Israel, Austin and I paid five shekels for crusty loaves of braided Sabbath bread—hollow like a drum when tapped, encrusted with sesame seeds that rained onto the floor. Along with the candles and *shalom*s of Shabbat evenings, challah consecrated the weekly day of rest.

After my dough rose, I rolled it into elastic ropes and braided two three-stranded loaves. I turned to challah-making to plow my heart—to remind myself of the humanity of Israelis and the beauty of the Jews' ancient culture and ancestral land. Living among Arabs, I find it embarrassingly easy to flatten them into stereotypes, to passively absorb generalizations made by my Palestinian neighbors. *Israelis are all rabid Zionists, all colonizing settlers. They all hate us.*

Making challah will help me remember my Israeli neighbors, with whom we sang and prayed on Saturday mornings: Ayelet, with voluptuous curls, strumming the guitar; Arie Bar-David illustrating the Scriptures with anecdotes from the Six-Day War; Tsuriel, serious-faced, righteous, and earnest, like a prophet. Challah will remind me of a tiny Messianic village on a pine-covered ridge, a place where I learned to chat in Hebrew and was shaped by the spiritual rhythms and texts of a nation.

I want to keep my heart toward Israelis soft, but I also hope challah might help me braid together the strands of my life. As an American evangelical, I was raised in a political and religious environment that favors Israeli perspectives, often conflating support for the Jewish people with support for the State of Israel. Until I moved beyond the Jordan, I wasn't well-acquainted with Palestinians and their stories.

Now I regularly hear about injustices the Jewish state has inflicted on my friends' and neighbors' relatives, both dead and alive. And I want to know: Can I harmonize the narratives dwelling inside me? On a personal level, can I reconcile the two streams of stories flowing through me, though Middle Eastern nations seem unable to make peace?

Intuitively, I reach for challah, on a hunch that baking bread might help.

* * *

Two weeks before October 7, I sit beside two Israelis on a flight from Amman to New York City. The young men are likely Mizrahi, Jews of Middle Eastern descent. Their kippa-covered hair and the stubble on their faces are dark like those of the Arabs around us. Noam, with a hawkish nose, speaks English better than Eli, who's a bit tubby and wears sweats and a T-shirt with the fringes of his inner prayer garment dangling.

It's a few hundred dollars cheaper to fly to NYC from Amman than from Tel Aviv, Noam tells me. He and Eli try to attend a Sukkot celebration in Brooklyn every year.

"Chag sameach," I say. *Happy holiday. Happy Feast of Booths.*

Eli and Noam break into smiles at my rough Hebrew, loosen up a bit more when I explain that I lived in Israel for two years.

"How is it traveling in Jordan?" I ask.

"We've not gone outside the airport," Noam states. "It wouldn't be safe for us."

Before our flight, Eli and Noam had been praying in the airport, wrapped in their striped prayer shawls with bits of the Torah strapped to their arms and foreheads. An Arab man approached them, shouting hatefully. When the Jews informed an airport security guard, he just laughed at them.

Something inside me flickers at their mistreatment, at the lack of respect they received from a Jordanian. Whenever that spark lights in me, I thank God. Thank him I haven't been hardened against wrong, regardless of the perpetrator.

* * *

Blessed are the poor in spirit, for theirs is the kingdom of heaven.

Blessed are those who mourn, for they shall be comforted.

Blessed are the meek, for they shall inherit the earth.

Blessed are those who hunger and thirst for righteousness, for they shall be satisfied.

Blessed are the merciful, for they shall receive mercy.

Blessed are the pure in heart, for they shall see God.

Blessed are the peacemakers, for they will be called sons of God.

* * *

On October 7, 2023, the morning after the end of Sukkot, around 5,000 militants led by Hamas break through the security fence between southern Israel and the Gaza Strip. They plow through the chain-link and barbed wire using explosives and bulldozers. Others fly over using go-karts rigged with paragliders. Israeli communities such as Kibbutz Be'eri and Kafr Aza are ransacked, burned. An overnight music festival in the Negev is ravaged.

Around 1,200 Jews are killed that day, more than any single day since the Nazis butchered them in death camps. Men, women, and children from border communities are trundled away on motorcycles and in pickup trucks, the oldest eighty-six, the youngest nine months. The media adjusts hostage counts day after day—120, more than 200, 240, 251.

In the early morning hours, thousands of rockets soar into Israel from Gaza. Most are intercepted by the Iron Dome defense system in an awful, cosmic game of cat and mouse. From Amman, I message an acquaintance in our former village. She says she can feel each blast in her chest. She and her daughters spend hours in the community bomb shelter, a concrete structure with a heavy metal door, cool inside like a cellar or a morgue.

In ways, Hamas's attack does not surprise me. In 2023, Israeli forces and settlers killed 243 Palestinians in the West Bank, more than any other year in decades. While washing dishes at night, Austin and I had mulled the possibility of a third intifada for months.

But this attack—this flood, this hurricane, this murderous wave of evil—we didn't expect this. We read the news and feel dread in our stomachs like lead. Prime Minister Netanyahu, leading the most far-right government in Israel's history, insinuates that Hamas's assault will alter the face of the Middle East.

I've lived through more than one war between Israel and Hamas, but already I know this will not be a "normal" war. On a societal level, collective memories and trauma have been triggered in Israelis, people I lived among and loved. This, I sense, will lead to a no-holds-barred decimation of Gaza, the ruin of 2.3 million Palestinians to whom my heart is bound.

* * *

On that same flight from Amman to New York City, an elderly Palestinian woman, Um Mahmoud, sits behind me. Unable to decipher the information on her seat-back screen, she asks me partway through the flight how many hours remain. I inform her, then crouch in the aisle and introduce her to David and Adam. She pinches my cheek and commands me to have a girl.

She was born in Yaffa, she tells me when I inquire, and was carried as a baby to Jordan during the Nakba in 1948. "The Jews took our land," she says.

I see lament deep in her eyes, recognizing it from conversations with other Palestinians. And my mind can hardly absorb how I am flying 560 miles per hour above the earth surrounded by hundreds of Arabs and a couple of dozen Israelis. No one seems to acknowledge this, no one seems to be talking, except the flight attendants using sterilized, neutral English as they serve piles of half-frozen kosher meals before carts of piping-hot halal ones. Here I am, shuttling between two peoples, switching languages and cultures like an ambassador, a bridge-builder.

When my row-mate Eli stands to open the overhead bin, Um Mahmoud asks him a question. He hovers above her, hairy arms lifted to grab his bag. She doesn't recognize the tassels sticking out below his T-shirt, the black kippa on his head. She just hollers at him in Arabic.

"English?" he says abashedly, staring down at her.

I crane my neck and over the airplane's roar shout back. "He doesn't speak Arabic."

I don't mention what he does speak.

* * *

Those who respond to the call and agree to carry and love what God loves—which is both the good and the bad—and to pay the price for its reconciliation within themselves, these are the followers of Jesus Christ.

—Richard Rohr

* * *

A couple days after October 7—the launch of what Hamas calls al-Aqsa Flood—I watch a video posted by a Palestinian acquaintance of an IDF soldier being dragged away by an al-Qassam fighter. The look on the Israeli's face is raw terror, desolation, abandonment. The Arabic splayed across the bottom of the screen reads, "Al-Aqsa Flood will have no mercy."

Sitting in the back of a yellow taxi, I immediately feel sick. Someone I knew—a woman with small children—was rejoicing in this evil. How could she celebrate? How could she and so many others boast in Hamas's attack? With the force of a bomb, I encounter a flaw in the people to whom I'm tied by the Arabic language and God-placed love. Seventy-five years of displacement and oppression have warped some of their views and values.

I can't sleep. No one in the Middle East can sleep. More than once, when the call to prayer ripples across Amman, I am already awake, grieving and praying. My interior feels like a chalkboard with nails skittering over it. My hair begins to fall out from stress. For the first time since I had PTSD in 2016, my adrenal glands ache, two coals on top of my kidneys. I ponder the words of Richard Rohr, sent to me by an Israeli-American friend earlier this year. Is the anxiety I feel in my body the price of reconciliation he mentions?

As I read a spectrum of news sources, I feel destabilized by my knowledge of both sides. I understand the reasoning behind Hamas's atrocious attack; it was unconscionable, but I recognize it as desperate, violent resistance to the ongoing deprivation of Palestinian rights. At the same time, I can rationalize the tactical necessity of Israel's bombardment of Gaza, an urban area where average Palestinians are governed by extremists. Eliminating terrorists is necessary for the security of Israeli citizens. How could a nation of Jews live securely beside a group that has pledged to destroy them?

As a human being, I want to avoid ambiguity and align with one side. Israelis or Palestinians—with whom should I sympathize? I strain over Christ's difficult command—"Love your enemies, pray for those who persecute you"—especially as every hour, the enemy morphs and flip-flops in my mind. How am I supposed to love all—Arabs, Jews, even terrorist "monsters" who I cannot believe are beyond the reach of God's mercy?

Refusing to demonize either side, my chances of being misunderstood skyrocket. An Israeli friend asks if I'm condoning both-sideism. When I tell a Palestinian friend I reject Hamas's violence, she stops replying to my messages.

How do I feel? Pulled? Strained? Trapped in the middle? I envision my arms stretched horizontally and brutally nailed to a beam of wood.

Crucified. That's it.

I feel crucified between two peoples God created. Hung and bleeding between two peoples over whom he weeps.

* * *

The man under his fig tree telephoned the man under his vine:
"Tonight they definitely might come. Assign
positions, armor-plate the leaves, secure the tree, tell
the dead to report home immediately."

The white lamb leaned over, said to the wolf:
"Humans are bleating and my heart aches with grief.
I'm afraid they'll get to gunpoint, to bayonets in the dust.
At our next meeting this matter will be discussed."
All the nations (united) will flow to Jerusalem
to see if the Torah has gone out. And then,
inasmuch as it's spring, they'll come down
and pick flowers from all around.
And they'll beat swords into plowshares and plowshares
into swords, and so on and so on, and back and forth.
Perhaps from being beaten thinner and thinner,
the iron of hatred will vanish, forever.

—Yehuda Amichai

* * *

On October 9, I make challah because my meal plan, written before October 7, calls for it. It feels predetermined, ordained for me by an inscrutable God. Suddenly, my exploration of reconciliation is no longer a game but a frighteningly urgent necessity.

I am angry. Only two days in, and Israel has ordered a complete siege of Gaza—no food, water, or fuel to the enclave that usually receives 500 trucks of aid daily. Already I have seen white-shrouded bodies of Palestinian children—so much like these oiled strands of dough—killed in retaliatory Israeli strikes.

In the first week, my neighbor's family grieves the death of more than forty relatives. In the first month, a Gazan woman I know in Jordan reports that her family's apartment building has been destroyed. In the courtyard after church one autumn morning, a friend describes how all her male relatives, sleeping in a first-floor apartment, were gunned down by an IDF tank. One of them was a doctor at al-Shifa Hospital. He studied in Jordan and returned to Gaza to serve his people.

From where she is sheltering in a church complex in Gaza City, a Palestinian Christian woman named Hannah contacts an American friend of mine, also living in Amman. *The people of Jesus are heartbroken and waiting for healing and peace,* she messages. *We want to live. I cry while I write this because my people, people who have nothing to do with politics or violence, are burned, broken, and heartbroken.*

Hannah becomes my human connection to Gaza. I pray for her often, my sister in faith, less than one hundred miles away. When the sun breaks out in Amman, I think of her hanging her laundry in the church's courtyard or sitting in the sun to warm herself. When it rains, I imagine her huddled on a mattress in a classroom of the church's school with her two kids. Outside, sheets of rain create tacky, clinging mud.

* * *

Two weeks after October 7, King Abdullah speaks at a peace summit in Cairo. Seated behind a spray of white roses, he addresses other delegates in English. He squints his blue eyes often—I guess he's weary like me—and mourns the acts of violence committed against citizens in Gaza, the West Bank, *and* Israel. He refuses to rejoice like some other Arabs.

The Hashemite king, a descendant of the Prophet Mohammad, speaks of Jews, of Israelis as equals, as "people of the Middle East." Hamas, on the other hand, along with many

Arab news outlets, does not deign to call Israelis what they are. They refer to them as "the occupation" or "the aggressor," as if the word "Israeli" would dirty their mouths. They put Israel in quotation marks, as if the country only exists in peoples' imaginations.

King Abdullah shares his vision for a secure future, including "two states, Palestine and Israel, sharing land and peace from the river to the sea." My heart swells when I hear his brave and inclusive choice of words. Hamas and other resistance movements use the phrase "from the river to the sea" to describe a land "liberated" from Jews. Jordan's monarch just turned that on its head and conjured up a place for both.

I feel like I'm listening to a prophet. He casts a vision for a peaceful future, moderately but firmly calling the world to do justice and love mercy. He does criticize Israeli military actions in Gaza, cuttingly, but didn't the biblical prophets criticize the people of Israel too? Men like Isaiah, Jeremiah, Micah, and Amos didn't speak to an irreproachable people. They rebuked the Israelites when they committed injustice and iniquity, when they oppressed the poor, the foreigners in their midst, the widows and orphans. When violence was found in the streets of Jerusalem, they condemned it. They did not flinch from the message God prepared for them; they opened their mouths wide and spoke the word of the LORD.

As the days of war march on, I wonder if I might have a prophetic role too. Alongside the role of reconciler, do I have the right to lovingly confront and point out the sins of others in hopes that they will repent and live? Can I call out Israeli passivity, how so many living in the Holy Land seem ignorant of Palestinian history, how they sideline the voices of 5 million non-Israeli Arabs in Gaza and the West Bank? Can I point out how every war results in what seems an overuse of military force? Can I chide the government when it authorizes settlements on Palestinian land? Can I rebuke the binding fear that leads those in power to deny the rights of average Palestinians in the name of security?

And I can be a prophet for both sides, right? I can call out the way many Palestinians perpetuate bitterness in their children, how they lack the ability to compromise. I can reprove those who glorify martyrs who die while committing evil in the name of resistance. I can admonish those whose desire for honor prevents them from admitting wrong and condemn the lust for land that drives radicalism and violence.

And though some of my Arab friends are aligning with Hamas, I won't exclude the group from my call. I hate their syrupy propaganda. I hate how their fighters are so insidiously intertwined under, around, and above Gaza like a bloated python, how they headquarter and hide in hospitals and schools, how they get civilians killed and then blame Israel. I hate how they mutilated and raped Israeli women on October 7 but officially deny it. Can I condemn Hamas for these atrocities while at the same time weeping for average Gazans who are forced to bear their punishment?

These thoughts pile up inside me as Arabs boycott U.S.-made products and protest American complicity in the war after Friday's noontime prayers. When I leave my house, I wear my black scarf embroidered with bold red Palestinian patterns, a type of fire insurance. Outwardly, I appear pro-Palestinian. In my kitchen, though, where no one can see me, I make challah, faithfully carving space for the enemy in my heart.

* * *

Wars will not heal our land or our souls or our pain. Killing our neighbor will not resolve our problems. We need instead the courage of peace. We need peace in which Palestinians and Jews can live together in equality and justice. We need peace that overcomes ethnic differences. We need the peace of Jesus Christ, the vision of a kingdom in which "he himself is our peace" and has "put to death [our] hostility."

—Yohana Katanacho,
Palestinian-Israeli theologian

* * *

I don't pray only for Hannah after October 7. I scrutinize pictures of IDF soldiers who died in combat, hoping I don't recognize them. I think of Tami and Uri on their land with pomegranate blossoms and bee boxes; of Israel and Audeline and our adventure to Haifa more than a decade ago; of Yochanan, our former neighbor with stormy eyes and a widow's peak. I pray for them though I lost contact with them all years ago.

I pray for Amitay, a soldier from a Messianic family. When his unit entered a residential building in Gaza to dismantle a Hamas tunnel, a remotely activated bomb exploded. Amitay was transported by helicopter to an Israeli hospital where both his legs were amputated.

Some days, I no longer know what to pray, besides vague cries for quiet, for peace. I return to words I learned as a child:

> Our Father in heaven,
> Hallowed be your name.
> Your kingdom come, your will be done,
> on earth as it is in heaven.

Austin and I pray the words before meals and together in the dark when it's all too much and we feel like we're living at the end of the world. David prays them in song form because he's learning the Lord's Prayer for Arabic class. We listen to recordings until Adam is singing a convoluted version of the first line too.

One night, David asks me to sing it before he goes to sleep— *Abana alladhi*. I lie on the bottom bunk with him above me, and together we sing. I think of Hannah, how she might sing this to her children. I think of Amitay, who might lose an eye in addition to his legs. I recall a therapist's words to me: *You are courageous because you choose to believe in the face of all you've seen.*

I try to believe, try to reconcile an invisible, sovereign God who declares himself merciful with the cruel, burning world scorched on my eyes through news articles and social media posts. I climb my watchtower, trying to rise above the mushroom clouds of smoke to find him.

* * *

Israelis start to count time based on the days their hostages have been in captivity. So on the 105th of October, which is late December 2023, I make challah again. Adam drags the stepstool across the tile and peers at me while I roll the dough into three snakes.

"Mama, you're making the challah?" he cries happily, pronouncing his *ch* heavy like an Arab.

"Yes, buddy, I'm making challah. Do you remember in which country they eat challah?"

"Umm," he thinks aloud. "Challah is good."

"In Israel," I say, intentionally speaking the word we do not speak in public. "They eat challah a lot there."

He runs away as I tuck in the ends of the braid and set the loaf on a pan. I place it in front of the gas heater in the living room, where a single strand of white lights frames our window. Across the West Bank and Jordan, public Christmas celebrations have been cancelled, a collective sign of lament for the Palestinians in Gaza. It feels appropriate. The land where Christ was born bleeds—why shouldn't we strip down our festivities when the people he came to redeem are still lost and rebellious, still not reconciled to God and thus unable to reconcile with each other?

Most don't want to talk about reconciliation, not now, while nerves are raw and bombs still falling. More and more, reconciliation feels like a miraculous third way, a hard, gritty miracle that requires the intervention of God's spirit to pursue. On Christmas night, an Iraqi friend reminds me that people who choose this way are often maligned and misunderstood. "In Iraq, people called Christians cowards because they didn't take revenge," she told me. "'I don't forgive because I love you,'" she'd explain to revilers, "'but because of my love for Christ who commanded me to forgive.'"

247

I remember Hannah's words from early in the war: *We are peaceful Christians and reject violence from both sides. Love, as Christ taught us, is the effective weapon for peace.* Since she sent those lines, the wall of the church where she's sheltering has been damaged by rocket fire. The presence of IDF snipers forced the believers to remain inside for days, motionless. The church's electric panels were destroyed, cutting off power to fifty-four disabled people on ventilators. Still: *We reject violence. Love is the weapon for peace.*

I keep a picture I saw on social media in my mind's eye: two small boys walking down a road. The one on the left wears a hoodie that's green, red, white, and black like the Palestinian flag. The one on the right wears a matching sweatshirt bearing the blue Star of David. Between them, holding their hands and leading them toward the future, is Jesus.

* * *

I meet with a Jordanian Muslim friend who has struggled with insomnia and illness since October 7. "My body refuses what is happening," she tells me as we eat *shakshuka* and bread with cheese and za'atar. We admit that we feel guilty sometimes about eating when people in Gaza are scrounging for food. We discuss the news in detail, concluding that when the Messiah returns, he will judge rightly, exposing and punishing evil and vindicating those who have done right. We feel grateful for a scrap of sure, shared hope.

Later, I meander through a village west of Amman and reflect on this hope. The early morning air smells like goats and the dew-soaked, decomposing grasses under oak scrub.

I pass a man banging olives onto a plastic tarp, with fluty music coming from the phone in the back pocket of his jeans. When I see the western horizon, belted by smog, I sit beside an old limestone cistern. The sky is a taut square of blue silk above me.

I stare toward the West Bank and wonder how literal the promises and prophecies about Jerusalem will be. All that talk about a city where absolute justice and righteousness reign— will it be an actual brick-and-mortar metropolis in the land next door, or do the prophets employ it as a symbol of an eternal kingdom? John's apocalyptic visions—the scrolls and trumpets and beasts—are those just metaphors? Do the details matter as long as restoration occurs?

As the sun rises, light smooths the texture from the wadis and brown hills. Multi-story apartment buildings become blinding and flat. All around me, skeletal thistles and dead plants create a palette of browns. Dry grasses catch photons of light in their papery husks. Do I really believe that redemption will come to this region? Can I still trust that, like plants in spring, a renewed version of this land and its peoples will rise?

I do. This is the story I tell myself in order to live. Day after day, I preach to myself, *This is not the end. Resurrection is coming. Redemption and renewal are coming.* Whether he actually arrives on a white horse, Christ will come and make all things new. He will wipe away my tears, mend my griefs, and make everything right. Wars will end, peace will flourish, a new order will emerge with the Messiah as king.

"Evangelism is the proclamation of the New," writes artist Makoto Fujimara.

If he's right, I'm the fiercest evangelist in the Middle East.

* * *

> Real peace is not between governments but between individuals who discover that they have the same worries, the same concerns, that they have suffered in the same way, and that there is something they can both put into creating a relationship that would benefit all of them.
>
> —King Hussein of Jordan

* * *

By February 2024, I'm watching 1.9 million Gazans trapped in Rafah, the one place Israel told them to flee for safety. After defeating Hamas in Gaza City, the IDF divided southern Gaza into more than 200 blocks, purportedly so they could inform Palestinians when their buildings were targeted by shelling. NGO workers call it a turkey shoot.

Now Israel says they'll bring the battle to Rafah, where already displaced Palestinians are strangled and starved and panicked. And—curse my nimble, capacious mind—I understand the need to pursue Hamas there, even as the other half of me screams, *Hamas isn't going to die—it's an ideology, not a person!* "This war on Gaza will not bring us security," writes Yuval Abraham, an Israeli journalist and activist. "Even if we topple Hamas, by killing so many Palestinian civilians, we will create the next Hamas."

I'm reading the poet Rainer Maria Rilke with harrowing images of mummy-like, shrunken faces in my mind. Pictures of Palestinians trampled and shot while trying to acquire food from aid convoys. Children eating donkey feed, grass, and dry cat food. Seventy percent of Gaza's housing wrecked. Three hostages shot by IDF soldiers, even though they were holding a white cloth and calling for help in Hebrew. Two-hundred thousand Israelis displaced. The equivalent of more than a soccer stadium full of Palestinians dead.

> Since I still don't know enough about pain,
> this terrible darkness makes me small.

I lie flat on my back on the floor, my palms upturned and open. I want the Almighty, this riddle of a God, to find me when he reaches for me. I want to keep after him like Job, like Habakkuk, like David and Jesus—all these Jews who taught me to pray.

> Shall we receive good from God, and not trouble?
> God thunders wondrously with his voice,
> he does great things we cannot comprehend.
> These are but the outskirts of his ways,
> and how small a whisper do we hear of him.

Their words and examples are my spiritual heritage. I'm grafted in from a wild olive tree—rooted in an ancient way and yet part of something fresh. I'm a citizen of a new, other-worldly kingdom whose principles and foundations eclipse the old. I live in an era where God so loves the world, where chosen ones are determined by their faith.

But if God loves us all, then why this pain?

> If it's you . . .
> press down hard on me,
> break in that I may know the weight of your hand,
> and you, the fullness of my cry.

In my place of surrender on the living room floor, tears wander from my eyes to my temples. *Keep listening to the thunder of his voice,* Job exhorts.

I lie still and listen.

* * *

I'm going to keep saying Psalm 150 every day. . . . I'm going to keep doing that because Psalm 150 is going to happen. We are going to be joyous, and we are going to feel just absolutely over the moon when . . . all the hostages get home . . . I'm tired, I'm sad, I'm disappointed, but I'm hopeful. Hope is mandatory.

—Rachel Goldberg,
mother of hostage Hersh Polin-Goldberg

* * *

On the 150th day of this madness, when my body is again fizzing with anxiety, I make challah—honey-wheat like I did a month ago, a round, wreath-like braid. I knead and try to pray, wanting to see those hostages released, wanting to see a ceasefire before Ramadan so the Middle East's lid doesn't blow off.

While the bread bakes, I sit on a stool, reading articles about challah-making. Apparently it wasn't my idea to repair soul damage through pliable dough. For many observant Jewish women, baking challah is a spiritual task as well. I read about women crying into their dough as they pour out their hearts to God, women seeking solutions, pleading for mercy, supplicating the Almighty for intervention, reaffirming their commitment to believe and obey.

In the Torah, the Hebrew word *challah* refers to a portion of dough women were commanded to remove from their mixing bowls and burn, like a sacrifice. Observant Jewish women still do this—they pinch off golf-ball sized portions and blacken them in pieces of tin-foil, dedicating their bread and their lives to the Lord.

What did I read in the Psalms this week? "I will offer to you the sacrifice of thanksgiving." Can I offer praise even when I don't understand God's purposes, even as Houthis target shipping in the Red Sea and Hezbollah lobs rockets from Lebanon into Galilee and babies die from malnutrition in Gaza? Though he slay me, will I trust him?

I think about Jewish women baking challah, and I imagine Palestinian women making bread in Gaza. I've seen pictures of huge bags of flour supplied by aid groups, of women sitting in the rubble beside soot-blackened stoves. Women putting one foot in front of another, waiting on God for their daily bread. *Alhamdulillah*, they say, the right response to every question. *Thanks be to God, who we believe is here, even in this mess.*

Maybe there will be a ceasefire this week, maybe not. I honestly don't know how to pray for it anymore. But someday this will end. When it does, everyone living in the Middle East will walk out of the wreckage battered and sore, some of us disfigured by trauma, missing literal limbs, others changed by months of psychological wrestling.

What are those lines by Mahmoud Darwish?

> I become someone else—transfigured.
> Words sprout like grass from Isaiah's prophetic mouth:
> "If you do not believe, you will not be safe."
> I walk as if I am someone else.
> And my wounds are white gospel flowers
> and my hands are like two doves
> on the cross, hovering and carrying the earth.

I will continue to praise and hope and believe, persistent as the prophets. When the possibility of peace emerges, I'll be ready, my arms extended toward both sides. Cautious but courageous, I will move into the holy wasteland. I will step into the gap with my hands stretched out like these broken doves.

BENEDICTION

Postcard from the Lowest Place on Earth

We talked the other day, and I told you, "We're going to the Dead Sea," and you said, "You're going to float!" and I thought, *No, that's not why we go.*

I only swam in the Dead Sea once, in 2006, and I stung in all the places chafed from hiking. Since then I have been content to watch other people swim. I derive endless amusement from observing bikini- and Speedo-clad tourists bob in the waters. Buoyed up like capsized frogs they float, joyfully cruciform in the saline waters of the lowest spot on earth. What a comic parade of pink-skinned people covering themselves with mineral-rich mud! What indecencies the patient lifeguards endure—the cleavage, the wedgie-picking, the undressing! (What do they go home and tell their mothers and sisters, their jealous wives?)

No, I do not equate the Dead Sea with floating. Palatial resorts come to mind, the sound of hundreds of moaning AC units, ironed white sheets and comforters, TVs with no English channels, just cartoons in classical Arabic. And breakfast buffets—five kinds of olives glistening in oil, cauldrons of foul, custom-made omelets and pancakes, cucumbers and tomatoes and yogurts, twists of cinnamon bread, croissants with za'atar or sticks of chocolate planted inside.

Of course, each family member has their thoughts. David dreams only of swimming—roasting the backs of his legs in the sapphire pools and getting red-raccoon eyes from his goggles, and Austin imagines Chedorlaomer of Elam running the kings of Sodom and Gomorrah into bitumen pits. To each his own.

After breakfast I spend an hour on the porch sipping Nescafé 3-in-1 while overlooking the sea and the wadi-carved mountains west of it. I'm not typically nostalgic, but here I give myself permission, space to the land that continually resurfaces in my dreams. (Why does it do that, come back and back and back— the neighbor who cannot stop calling?) Amidst the chatter of grackles and sparrows, the swooping of swifts and head-pumping of laughing doves, I look at the sea in the tectonic-clawed valley and the land of Canaan beyond.

Sometimes I walk down to the water—a long walk, as the sea recedes about a yard annually, its main sources diverted by Israel, Jordan, and Syria for household, agricultural, and industrial use. Hotels add stairways and boardwalks year by year to keep up. In 1896, the water's surface was 425 yards below sea level; now, in 2024, it's 478 yards. As the water recedes, sink holes form, cutting a treacherous shoreline. A logical turn of events for a region hailed as Sodom and Gomorrah perhaps, but tough for the tourism business. I've heard talk about bringing water from the Red Sea to prevent the Dead Sea from shrinking farther. "They've been saying that for twenty-five years," says Abu Saif, one of the lifeguards.

I stand in the water, breathe the oxygen-rich air. Nearby rocks resemble grade-school crystal-growing projects—the rim where water meets land is iced with salt. When I dip in my hands and feet, I feel like they're coated with light oil. Abu Saif helps me begin to list the minerals in the water, many of which are harvested from evaporation pans by Jordanian and Israeli companies in the sea's southern basin. Bromine, magnesium, potassium. The mud contains many more. Together they can alleviate skin conditions and arthritis. I wonder at how a place hailed by three religions as a place of destruction—blasted by sulfur and brimstone—has become a place of healing.

These opposing themes—ecological collapse and subversive redemption—bring me to the main thing I think about at the Dead Sea. I always read Ezekiel's vision here, which describes an ever-deepening river that will issue from Jerusalem, flow east, and enter the Dead Sea. It's an obscure vision recorded by a kooky prophet who also saw wheels covered in eyes and lay on his side for hundreds of days and ate bread baked over cow dung.

And perhaps I'm a bit crazy myself, because my soul contracts and I want to cry when I read that at the end of all things, these waters will become fresh and "there will be very many fish." Ezekiel saw trees along the river producing different fruits every month, and he says they'll have healing leaves, and something in me stirs deep and tells me this is the place of which another prophet said, "They will see his face."

When I visit the Dead Sea, I want to tell everyone about Ezekiel's vision, even Abu Saif the lifeguard. He of all people ought to know, he who has sat by this sea for thirteen years guiding foreign women into the waters and painting their faces with mud. I tell him about the prophecy, that after the Messiah comes and after the Day of Resurrection, the waters here will become pure. He looks at me thoughtfully, dark face and mustache under his red ball cap, accent suggesting he grew up in this valley. They don't have that story in Islam, he says, but there's one about the Sea of Galilee drying up before the Messiah kills the antichrist. I wonder if he believes my tale or if I seem off my rocker. He gives me a pendant-shaped clump of salts, and we part with blessings.

Tonight, while the Dead Sea lies before me, I watch the sky turn apricot and blue, the *hilal* the slenderest toenail over the churning sea and the glittering bank of Canaan magnetic as always—Ramallah, Jerusalem, and Bethlehem on the ridge, Jericho, Mizpeh Shalem, Mizpeh Qedem, and Ein Gedi lower down. Mahmoud Darwish comes to mind: "Our land, in its bloodied night, / is a jewel that glimmers for the far upon the far." I think about how the distance between me and that land is shrinking, how I'll swim here and play here and reign here forever.

Away from Amman's noise, I meditate on these promises again, engulfed by their magic, a current drawing me toward ultimate redemption. Belief is my vocation, I'm reminded, clinging to faith my greatest work. Wind ruffles the waters—or is it the hovering Spirit, the hand of God himself? And I am waiting, still on the lookout for the kingdom, imperceptibly but steadily blossoming in the ashes of apocalypse.

Swimmers ascend from the beach, speaking a variety of languages. If I could speak a thousand tongues, I could tell them about Ezekiel's prophecy too. I could grab their arms, gesture to all the land in sight, urge them to see the potential in this sun-blasted wilderness. "Will you believe me?" I'd say. "Will you believe me if I tell you this place will be changed—that renewal will come from this ruin, that this bloodied night will end? Will you believe me if I say that even this will be made new?"

About the Author

Heather M. Surls is an American writer who has lived in the Middle East for more than a decade. As an Arabic-speaking journalist, she is passionate about bridging cultural gaps and offering Western readers a deeper, more nuanced understanding of the region and its people. Through her creative nonfiction, she highlights women's voices and examines the interplay between place, culture, faith, and spirituality. She currently resides in Amman, Jordan, with her husband and two sons.

Acknowledgments

Many days, writing this book felt a solitary task. But the longer I wrote, the larger the community around me grew and the more I recognized the metaphorical foundation and support beams that enable me to write at all. I want to thank some of these pillars who've taught, trained, and held me up.

Grammy and Papa, two of my earliest and biggest cheerleaders—I wish you could hold this book in your hands.

Mom and Dad, who taught me to write—Mom by challenging my skills and making me read sometimes two novels a week, Dad by letting me type your letters to the newspaper editor and help refine your sentences.

Jack Simons, my college writing professor, who made me write reams in multiple genres and even stomped on my paper once for using "due to."

Terry Mattingly and the folks at Religion News Service, for honing my journalism skills.

Every website, journal, and magazine that's published my work, for giving me spaces to practice writing and keep my creative fire burning through early motherhood and international moves.

Elsa, Annie, Aylin, Theresa, and Elena, who offered constructive feedback on early chapters, and Libby, Mindy, Drew, Titus, and Hanadi, for your feedback and encouragement on my first full draft.

Rania, for caring for Adam twice a week for a year so I could focus on this project.

My tribe in Jordan, who encouraged me that writing a book was not selfish or sacrilegious and who cheered me on throughout the process. You know who you are.

Kami, for seeing stories everywhere with me, for praying for this project, and for telling me that writing a book at this point in my life would be "profoundly faithful."

Sarah, for your artist-hearted companionship and beautiful images to accompany my words.

Hashem, at our local office supply shop, who endured my many visits for printing individual chapters and then full manuscript drafts.

If I'm allowed to thank places and things, thank you to Rumi Café and Medusa's Guesthouse for being the best writing spots other than home, and Turtle Green Tea for being my caffeinated beverage of choice.

Beth, my perceptive editor who helped me solve problems in the manuscript no one else could—I now understand why authors gush about their editors.

The team at Lucid Books, for shepherding this first-time author with a niche audience and a hot potato of a book.

Every Arab mentioned in this work, for sharing your lives and friendship with a foreigner.

Rick and Becky, for embracing me as your daughter and supporting my work with enthusiasm.

David, who participated in many of these stories and endured my temporary obsessions with thobes, olives, bread, and everything else—you were a first reader and the first to write a review (for your fifth grade nonfiction book report). I love you.

Adam, who was also part of many of these stories, and who always reminded me that I have a body and am not just a disembodied writing brain—thank you for enduring a mama who is always a bit distracted. I love you too!

Lastly, and mostly, to Austin, who prioritizes my flourishing and personal goals in practical ways. Any achievements I've made, any success I find as a writer, are built on the foundation of your sacrificial, servant-hearted love.

𝔑otes

Invocation: The Desert Will Bloom

Jarir Maani's *Field Guide to Jordan* (2nd edition, Maani Publishing, 2010) has been a faithful companion on many an outdoor adventure here. All references to plants and birds in this book probably came from Maani.

The verses quoted are found in Isaiah 35:1–2, 6–7 (NIV).

Jessie van Eerden, *The Long Weeping* (Orison Books, 2017), 31, 33.

Liang Dan-Fong, *Jordan as I See: Land of Spiritual Wealth* (Ministry of Tourism & Antiquities, 1979), 12.

Perhaps Jordan's most recognizable symbol, the fringed, red-and-white checkered shemagh was adopted in the 1930s by the Desert Patrol, a Bedouin unit that guarded Transjordan's solidifying borders. Between 1948 and 1970, the headdress went out of fashion as King Hussein emphasized the unity of Jordan's east and west banks. But after Black September, when the Hashemites exiled the Palestinian Liberation Organization from the Kingdom, the shemagh resurfaced as a visual counterpoint to the black-and-white Palestinian keffiyeh. The scarf continues to represent Jordanian nationalism.

Bismillah

This prose-poem, along with the others beginning the four parts of this book, is a hybrid form known as a dervish essay. I'm grateful for Sophronia Scott's dervish piece "Autumn" in her essay collection, *Love's Long Line* (Mad Creek Books, 2018), which served as my first example of this form.

Tell Me a Better Way

The Psalms of Ascent are Psalms 120–134.

Sitting under a bush in the wilderness of Paran: Deuteronomy 8.

On a ridge in the wilderness of Tekoa, we read about Jehoshaphat: 2 Chronicles 20:20–23.

Whom have I on earth but you? Psalm 73:25 (ESV).

The Rachel Held Evans quote appeared in a *Relevant Magazine* article, "Why Faith Needs Doubt."

Behold, I will allure her: Hosea 2:14–15 (ESV).

Beyond the Jordan

The site I describe in *The Prayer Tree* is Mar Elias, traditional birth place of the prophet Elijah.

Story of Moses, Aaron, and Hur is recorded in Exodus 17:8–16.

As the deer pants for the water brooks: Psalm 42:1 (NASB).

A Portrait of Baghdad as Beautiful

"As long as the United States of America is determined and strong": speech by President George W. Bush to Congress and the American people, September 20, 2001.

"This will not be a campaign of half measures": speech by President Bush to the American people, March 19, 2003.

Sinan Antoon, "When I was torn by war," in *The Baghdad Blues* (Harbor Mountain Press, 2007).

The children's pictures are found in Mindy Belz's book, *They Say We Are Infidels: On the Run from ISIS with Persecuted Christians in the Middle East* (Tyndale House Publishers, 2016).

Maysoon's quote comes from the Qur'an, Surah Ya-Sin 36:9.

Slowly, Slowly

Naomi Shihab Nye, "Arabic," *19 Varieties of Gazelle: Poems of the Middle East* (Greenwillow Books, 2002), 90.

Attention

I wrote this dervish essay after a day in central Jordan—Moab of ancient times—including a visit to Makawir, probably the place where John the Baptist was imprisoned and beheaded.

I read this week that attention is prayer: This idea comes from "Attention and Will" in Simone Weil's book *Gravity and Grace*, translated from French to English in 1952.

Into the Rugged Unknown

Wilfred Thesiger, *Arabian Sands* (Longmans, 1959).

Jabril S. Jabbur, *The Bedouin and the Desert: Aspects of Nomadic Life in the Arab East* (State University of New York Press, 1995), 32.

Warp & Weft

Thank you to Brenda van den Brink and Abdullah al-Zwaydeh of Jordan Desert Journeys for organizing my weaving workshop with Um Ayman.

Proverbs 31:13, 17, 19, 25 (NIV).

Shelagh Weir, *The Bedouin* (British Museum Publications, 1990), 43.

Khalil Naouri, *Hands & Hearts: Weavings from Jordan*, 2013.

Alan Keohane, *Bedouin: Nomads of the Desert* (Trafalgar Square, 1994), 172–173.

Thank you to Sandra Jelly of Lumeyo for introducing me to the weaving women of Udhruh.

Table in the Wilderness

Elias Khoury, *Gate of the Sun*, English translation by Humphrey Davies (Archipelago Books, 2006).

I am the light of the world (John 8:12); *I am the bread of life* (John 6:35, ESV).

Yoav Alon, *Shaykh of Shaykhs: Mithqal al-Fayiz and Tribal Leadership in Modern Jordan* (Stanford University Press, 2016), 96.

Arab Folktales, translated and edited by Inea Bushnaq (Pantheon Books, 1986), 5.

Can God spread a table in the wilderness: Psalm 78:19 (ESV).

Qur'an, Surah al-Ma'idah 5:112–115, Arthur Arberry's translation.

Yet I Will Rejoice
Whispering to me Habakkuk's prayer: Habakkuk 3:17–19.

To sit quietly with the one core truth of the universe: Lamentations 3:21–33.

Sketches of Syrian Women
Talia's words come from Wendy Pearlman's book, *We Crossed a Bridge and It Trembled: Voices from Syria* (Custom House, 2018), 281.

Fear not, let not your hands grow weak: Zephaniah 3:16–17 (ESV).

Marie Brenner, "Marie Colvin's Private War," *Vanity Fair,* August 2012.

In repentance and rest is your salvation: Isaiah 30:15, 18 (NIV and CSB, respectively).

Yazin's surgery was successful, and he's now a healthy boy.

My Other Name Is Hagar

Hagar's story appears in Genesis 16 and 21. The Pauline passage mentioned is Galatians 4:21–31.

Ibrahim left Hajar and Ismail in the desert to "establish prayer": Qur'an, Surah Ibrahim 14:37.

Tamar Kadari, "Hagar: Midrash and Aggadah," *Shalvi/ Hyman Encyclopedia of Jewish Women*. March 20, 2009. Jewish Women's Archive, viewed on January 16, 2025, <https://jwa.org/encyclopedia/article/hagar-midrash-and-aggadah>.

Tony Maalouf, *Arabs in the Shadow of Israel* (Kregel, 2003).

How long, O LORD? Psalm 13:1 (ESV).

Riffat Hassan, "Islamic Hagar and Her Family," in *Hagar, Sarah, and Their Children,* edited by Phyllis Trible and Letty M. Russell (Westminster Knox Press, 2006).

Field Guide to the New Jerusalem

Good old Jarir Maani again. And Revelation.

With This Stitch, I Hope

This chapter would be possible without the instruction I received from Wafa Ghnaim's Village Series class on Palestinian embroidery and history. Wafa's book I refer to is *Tatreez & Tea: Embroidery and Storytelling in the Palestinian Diaspora* (2nd edition, 2018).

A thousand thanks to the staff of Tiraz Centre and to Widad Kawar for spending an hour with me in her home.

Widad Kamel Kawar, *Threads of Identity: Preserving Palestinian Costume and Heritage* (Rimal Books, 2011), from pages 8, 2, 22, respectively.

Hanan Munayer, lecture at the Library of Congress, 2012, https://www.loc.gov/item/webcast-5704/.

Walid Khalidi, All That Remains: The Palestinian Villages Occupied an*d Depopulated by Israel in 1948* (Institute for Palestine Studies, 2006).

Yanal Jbareen and Zena Abo Zkra, "Israel Plans to Build Villas on the Ruins of a Village That Has Become a Symbol of the Nakba," *Haaretz*, July 12, 2021, https://www.haaretz.com/israel-news/haaretz21/2021-07-12/ty-article-magazine/.premium/the-next-sheikh-jarrah-the-battle-for-palestinian-ruins-in-jerusalem-reawakens/0000017f-dc40-df62-a9ff-dcd7cff30000.

Hilda Granqvist, *Portrait of a Palestinian Village* (Third World Centre for Research & Publishing Ltd, 1981).

Palestine Royal Commission Report, 1937, and *Palestine Partition Commission Report,* 1938, both published in London by His Majesty's Stationary Office. The phrase "backward peasantry" appears on page 117.

Lena Khalaf Tuffaha, "Morning, Lantern," in *Letters from the Interior* (Diode Editions, 2019), 34.

A thousand thanks to Sara Jayyusi of Deerah and the women of al-Baqa'a, who allowed me to interview them.

These Common Threads
Thank you to India Hayford, who generously gave me her lecture, "Embroidery, Clothing, and Feminine Identity in Jewish Yemen," on Zoom.

I'm also grateful for *Yemenite Jewish Embroidery* by Margalit Adi-Rubin (M A R, 1983), which gave me historical background to write this short piece of fiction.

Braiding Challah
The Beatitudes appear in Matthew 5:3–10 (ESV).

Richard Rohr, "A Call to Awakening," Center for Action and Contemplation, January 12, 2023, https://cac.org/daily-meditations/a-call-to-awakening-2023-01-12/.

Yehuda Amichai, "Sort of an Apocalypse," *The Selected Poetry of Yehuda Amichai* (University of California Press, 2013).

King Abdullah speaks at a peace summit in Cairo, October 21, 2023.

Yohana Katanacho, "His Law Is Love and His Gospel Is Peace," *Christianity Today*, December 20, 2023, https://www.christianitytoday.com/2023/12/christmas-peace-israel-hamas-war-palestinian-christian/.

The Lord's Prayer: Matthew 6:9–10 (ESV).

This is the story I tell myself in order to live: This wording is taken from Joan Didion's essay "The White Album" in The White Album (4th Estate, 1979), 11.

Makoto Fujimara, *Art & Faith: A Theology of Making* (Yale University Press, 2020), 55.

King Hussein quoted from Avi Shlaim's *Lion of Jordan: The Life of King Hussein in War and Peace* (Penguin UK, 2009), 544.

Rainer Maria Rilke, "It feels as though I make my way through massive rock" from *Rilke's Book of Hours: Love Poems to God*, translated by Anita Barrows and Joanna Macy (Riverhead Books, 2005), 190–191.

This riddle of a God: The wording of this sentence comes from another poem in *Rilke's Book of Hours*, "You are not surprised," 133, 135.

Job 2:10 (NIV); 37:5 (ESV); 26:14 (ESV).

Rachel Goldberg on Instagram page bring.hersh.home, March 4, 2024.

I will offer to you the sacrifice of thanksgiving: Psalm 116:17.

Mahmoud Darwish, "In Jerusalem," *Do Not Apologize for What You Did* (Riad El-Rayyes Books S.A.R.L., 2004). This is my own translation from the Arabic. Original used by permission of the publisher.

Benediction: Postcard from the Lowest Place on Earth

Ezekiel's vision appears in Ezekiel 47 (ESV).

Another prophet said, "They will see his face": Revelation 22:4 (ESV).

These lines come from Mahmoud Darwish's poem, "To Our Land," which appears in *The Butterfly Garden* (Copper Canyon Press, 2008), translated by Fady Joudah and accessed through the Poetry Foundation.